Published in 2008 by Stewart, Tabori & Chang
An imprint of Harry N. Abrams, Inc.

Copyright © 2008 Szekely Family Foundation
Photographs copyright © 2008 by Robert Holmes

The name Rancho La Puerta® is a trademark owned by Indotel, S. de R.L de C.V.

Library of Congress Cataloging-in-Publication Data

Szekely, Deborah.
   Cooking with the seasons at Rancho La Puerta : recipes from the world-famous spa /
by Deborah Szekely and Deborah Schneider.
      p. cm.
   Includes index.
   ISBN 978-1-58479-709-8
   1. Cookery (Natural foods) 2. Cookery, Mexican. 3. Rancho La Puerta (Spa)
I. Schneider, Deborah M. II. Rancho La Puerta (Spa) III. Title.
   TX741.S937 2008
   641.5′636—dc22
                           2008007813

Editor: Luisa Weiss
Designer: Anna Christian
Production Manager: Jacquie Poirier

The text of this book was composed in Vendetta.

Printed and bound in China
10 9 8 7 6 5 4 3 2 1

HNA
harry n. abrams, inc.
a subsidiary of La Martinière Groupe

115 West 18th Street
New York, NY 10011
www.hnabooks.com

Cooking with the Seasons at
RANCHO LA PUERTA
RECIPES FROM THE WORLD-FAMOUS SPA

Deborah Szekely *and* Deborah M. Schneider

with Chef Jesús González, Chef of La Cocina Que Canta

STEWART, TABORI & CHANG ❧ NEW YORK

CONTENTS

INTRODUCTION

By Deborah Szekely

Food has been the driving force in my life. This was not completely my doing. My mother was vice president of the New York Vegetarian Society in 1926, when I was four years old. Bernarr Macfadden, the famous fitness fanatic and publisher, was also in the group and a friend of the family.

Lack of fresh fruits and vegetables during the Depression drove us out of a comfortable life in Brooklyn to a grass hut in Tahiti. There, as a twelve year old, I met my husband-to-be, although I certainly didn't realize it at the time. He was a health nut friend of my parents.

And so the course of my life was set.

After the fateful meeting in Tahiti, my energetic mother followed her new guru, Edmond Bordeaux Szekely, from Tahiti to San Francisco to Mexico to New Orleans, to Mexico (again). At sixteen, when my family journeyed to yet another Szekely health camp, I went to work as Edmond's secretary in Uruapan, Mexico. We had about five paying guests— his students from England. We grew coffee beans near a web of creeks

that fed a large river. If we were going to eat, I had to learn to cook, and I did—on a woodstove.

A year later on my way back to begin college, this helpless man (whom I adored) asked me to marry him and join him in England, where he was headed next as the director of the British International Health and Education Center.

But World War II changed everything. My husband's passport was cancelled. As a Jew and a reserve in the Romanian army, he couldn't go home; he was not about to fight on the side of Hitler. To make matters worse, the United States immigration authorities notified us that if he was found in the United States after June 1, 1940, he would be arrested as a deserter.

Together we crossed the border into Baja California, Mexico, and sought refuge. This is really where the story begins, at Rancho La Puerta, our health camp. Bring your own tent—$17.50 a week. When we opened, there were thirty-five guests who helped set up camp, climbed mountains, exercised in the river—and had to be fed!

We learned together, my guests and I. It was learning from the bottom up, the hard way, but the most effective way. There were lots of tears, and lots of successes. Three times a day our guests sat down at benches on long wooden tables under two arching oak trees and asked, "What's to eat?" And I realized that our food—so satisfying, so fulfilling—was becoming part of who I was. It became my leitmotif during hard times.

From the beginning we experimented. We read and discussed and tried every health discipline and diet theory you're still hearing about today: bean sprouts and acidophilus milk; total fasting and interval fasting; the grape cure; the mucus-free diet; morning walks; and mud baths. I have never come across anything that we didn't try once.

And so we began.

Between then and now there have been many meals, many recipes, and many books about food. Who needs another cookbook? Well, food is life, and I've learned a lot about food and a lot about life in these eighty-six years. Much is new. And much that is old now seems new because it's making a comeback. The most satisfying shift has been many cooks' return to finding and treasuring local food sources. Much of the country now has local, often organic food available at progressive grocery stores or increasingly popular farmers' markets. We are no longer considered heretics when we demand fresh, seasonal, local produce. This book will help you do your part in minimizing what is now called a product's carbon footprint—the environmental impact of the miles it traveled by fossil-fuel engines.

Over the decades, the food at Rancho La Puerta (as well as at its sister spa, the Golden Door, which I started in 1957) has played a vital role in our mission to strive for health and wellness through mind/body/spirit balance. Has it changed much over the years? Oh yes! Our North Star is the saying *siempre mejor* (always better), and there is little about our food today that would resemble that of the early days at the Ranch except for these two important factors: It was, and still is, fresh from the earth or sea; and it was, and still is, best prepared and enjoyed by those who understand the notion of the complete calorie.

Thirty years ago when I wrote the book *Secrets of the Golden Door* I said, "My goal will be to advise you how to pleasure yourself as you grow in your ability to balance your intake of proper food/fuel with your output of living energy. The secret, obviously, is to double your pleasure without doubling your calories, by emphasizing the psychological rather than the physical calorie. If you learn my lessons well, you'll have learned to discard your attitude of crime and punishment (i.e., the belief that it's a crime to eat, so you must punish yourself by dieting)."

This psychological calorie about which I wrote has become my complete calorie. The food we eat is complete only when we understand and find joy in the many facets of growing, purchasing, preparing, and enjoying it—preferably with family and friends. In recent years, the Slow Food Movement has been a godsend embraced by the culinary community, repurposing chefs', diners', and home cooks' approaches to the complete calorie. The movement's mission calls us to be stewards of the earth, supporters of small local farmers, seekers of freshness and taste, explorers in the kitchen (this book is your treasure map!), and hosts and hostesses of that most satisfying social custom of sharing a meal with friends.

This book will not only help you make good food, but also free you to enjoy it more. I love food. It is a life force. But our culture has caused us to be hemmed in by it and has made it a no-no when it should be one of the most positive and naturally balanced necessary pleasures in life.

My dearest hope is that you and your loved ones will use this book many times to enjoy simple and wonderful meals and discover a new lifestyle of the complete calorie.

As we say in Mexico: "*¡Salud!*"

ABOUT THIS BOOK

By Deborah Schneider

I want to state up front that this is not a diet book. No, for this book we are going for nothing less than changing your life, or at least changing how you think about food and how you cook—which in the end, you'll discover, is pretty much the same thing.

Chew on this: How you feel every day is directly related to what you put—or don't put—into your body. In this book, our goal is feeling good, full of energy, vitality, creativity and—Deborah's favorite word—joy. Food and cooking can be one of the great pleasures of your life. When you eat well and enjoy yourself, you'll feel better. Well-being is not just about living a long life. It's about feeling great for every beautiful, irreplaceable day of it.

Deborah Szekely has always been well ahead of her time, from her first proto-organic garden at the foot of Mount Kuchumaa to her staunch refusal, even in the heyday of the fad diet, to buy into the idea that food is the enemy. Deborah's philosophy was always about being well and feeling good rather than just dropping a dress size. She made it a point to make fresh, simple, organically grown food central to the Ranch experience. What she began was truly radical in the 1940s. Today, six decades later, chefs and consumers are waking up to the reality that if we don't move quickly to make changes to the way we produce and use food, we're in trouble both personally and globally.

INTO THE GARDEN

I visited Rancho La Puerta and Tres Estrellas for the first time in August 1986, when I ventured south for a day to visit my friend Joe Cochran, who was then chef at the Ranch. In the course of our tour we stopped by Tres Estrellas, where Deborah's daughter, Sarah Livia, had just started work on two acres of fallow Baja ranchland. Under the blazing August sun, Joe proudly pointed out a patch of carefully tilled earth and a few gangly saplings drooping in the stifling heat. He went into great detail about Sarah's master plan: hand-dug French intensive raised beds, all-organic composting, grass and clover paths—though on this day the few rows of greens seemed overwhelmed by the stony hillsides and relentless mountain winds. That afternoon, Joe's cooks scrubbed and peeled what looked like several thousand beets and picked over a few heads of heat-scorched lettuce. It was no surprise when beets appeared on my plate that night. What was surprising was that they were *delicious*.

Fast-forward twenty-five years, to my first exploratory visit as coauthor-to-be of a cookbook about the Ranch's new cooking school and culinary center, La Cocina que Canta. The windswept patch that had been Tres Estrellas was now a lush landscape of five acres, planted with alternating rows of fruit trees, herbs, and lettuce and vegetables. The stone-and-brick kitchen house was completely overrun with climbing roses and flowering vines. Bees thrummed by the thousands in head-high bushes of fragrant lavender and rosemary. Birds chirped. Hummingbirds hummed, and butterflies fluttered, as butterflies will, from leaf to flower. A worn wooden bench beckoned from the shade of a vast mulberry tree. In the open courtyard of La Cocina, a soothing fountain trickled. Mustachioed gardeners wheeled barrows heaped with colorful mountains of peppers, lettuces, herbs, tomatoes, squash, beets, celery, and leeks down the paths to be loaded up for a morning delivery just over the hill to the Ranch. The transformation was complete. Whatever was imaginary a quarter-century ago had put down roots and flung itself into being with joyous abandon. It was Eden, every chef's dream. Forget writing a book: I wanted to live here, and cook here, forever.

The experience of working with Chef Jesús González and Head Gardener Salvador Tinajero on this book has transformed me. It's been a subtle shift from seeing food not just as a product that comes out of a box, but as something that grew in a particular place in its appropriate season, tended by human beings. I can't bring myself to pronounce *terroir* properly (I sound like Barbara Walters), but I can surely taste the season in a ripe nectarine. I look at lettuce leaves individually, to better admire their shapes and colors. I know why supermarket carrots are bland, because over the years it took to research and write the book, I watched the gardeners dig, harrow, weed, compost, worry, and fret over their carrots. It takes love and dedication to make a carrot taste that good. Once I was recalibrated to what really good, fresh food tasted like, nothing else would do. I'm spoiled. Correction: I'm saved.

Things *have* changed. I prefer less oil and less salt and more beautiful fresh vegetables, fruits, and herbs. (I still can't imagine life without butter and chocolate, though.) A little at a time, I learned how to add a handful of veggies here and there to boost the nutritional value of what I cooked. I now prefer to use whole grains instead of white stuff. I make salads of roasted vegetables and herbs and snack on carrots and cranberries and almonds. I make lots of soups and exceptional organic bread to go with it, and my children eat it. In fact, they often make it. The sight of my daughter, with pierced nose and iPod, kneading bread by hand was one of those strange moments when I realized that the world was going to be okay after all, even if it looked different.

In the end, it comes down to the choices we make, and the things we do because we really care about something—a result, a philosophy, a belief. I see how hard Salvador and his team work in the garden and how passionate he is merely talking about what he grows and why. I watch Jesús, a natural teacher, lead his class back to their senses: touching, smelling, tasting, chopping, stirring, and enjoying. We remember how truly wonderful the very simplest things in our lives can be if approached with care and respect … and gratitude.

A CHEF AND A GARDENER

JESÚS GONZÁLEZ, CREATIVE CHEF, LA COCINA QUE CANTA

Creative Chef Jesús González says with a smile that he learned to cook "at the school of Mom." Señora González was (and still is) very particular about basic ingredients, insisting on the best and only the best. At her side, in the legendary markets of his native Mexico City, Jesús learned the same passionate focus on the quality of simple things.

With legendary Golden Door chef Michel Stroot as his next teacher, Jesús absorbed classic French technique. And with the Door's organic garden right outside the kitchen, he gained a respect for natural flavors and presentations, turning out meals that were fresh, beautiful, and healthy. Stroot came to trust him and let him experiment, allowing him to learn in the process about building and balancing flavors, texture, color, and taste, lessons that Jesús now incorporates into everything he teaches.

Jesús cooks in the traditional styles of Mexico and Europe, often without written recipes, relying instead on a knowledge of simple cooking techniques and his own tastes and instincts. These are the same skills that he strives to impart to his students at La Cocina Que Canta: Choose the best ingredients, treat them with respect, and taste what you cook. Understanding flavor is so important that he conducts frequent impromptu tastings of herbs, tomatoes, and other treats from the garden so that students can learn to taste the differences.

"A recipe is just the beginning of cooking," Jesús explains. "Tasting is everything. Everything! My students learn to taste and adjust recipes as they cook, because ingredients can change."

"It might seem like a limitation, to work only from what we grow," he says, "but it really is limitless. The garden is incredible—it is the best

JESÚS GONZÁLEZ

thing—there is so much of everything that my imagination goes wild."

SALVADOR TINAJERO, HEAD GARDENER, TRES ESTRELLAS

It's easy to idealize what farmers and gardeners do. The truth is that the year is long, the work is hard, and the results can be heartbreaking. Gardeners are not so much artists as they are stubborn managers of that ultimate diva, *la madre natural*. But Nature, sometimes generous and sometimes savagely capricious, does not always cooperate.

SALVADOR TINAJERO

A chef wants consistency and predictability from his garden, and tiny baby vegetables, all the same size, delivered when he wants them. Tres Estrellas head gardener Salvador Tinajero always wants to grow new things in the garden, just to see what will happen. A poet of plants, he can list ten kinds of carrots and a dozen or more of types of tomatoes and describe the finer qualities of each with precision and the enthusiasm of an aficionado.

Salvador firmly believes that plants have personalities. Radicchio, for example, "likes lots of elbow room." Salvador is known as "*el rey del ajo y chiles*," the king of garlic and chiles. And he is, growing half a dozen kinds of pungent garlic and many more kinds of lovely (and sometimes lethally hot) chiles, just to see how different seeds and species respond to the Tres Estrellas microclimate. If Jesús is an artist, Salvador is an explorer. He works not to conquer, but to mediate between the chef and nature, and perhaps to discover something new and wonderful.

THE VISIONARY

SARAH LIVIA BRIGHTWOOD, OWNER, TRES ESTRELLAS

Sarah Livia Brightwood, the daughter of Deborah Szekely, is the owner, designer, and creative force behind Tres Estrellas, the organic farm that provides many of the fruits and vegetables to the Ranch. She is the president of Rancho La Puerta and, with her formal training in landscape design, has overseen the landscape designs at the Ranch for the past twenty years. Under Sarah's leadership, Rancho La Puerta has launched many innovative programs in conservation, sustainable agriculture, low-water use landscapes, and the use of native plants. The Ranch has long been considered a leader in green destination spa programs.

She is the president of Fundacion La Puerta, a not-for-profit family foundation started by the Szekely family and former Ranch partner José Manuel Jasso, dedicated to natural history education for Tecate school children and their teachers. It supports a number of conservation and cultural programs that serve the people of Tecate and the cross-border region. Sarah and the Fundacion were instrumental in setting aside two thousand of the Ranch's three thousand total acres as a nature preserve in perpetuity—a bold stroke that was key to the establishment of a large cross-border wildlife corridor in consort with the United States Bureau of Land Management, Mexico's Pronatura, and other conservation organizations.

Also a talented artist and writer, Sarah brings her creative eye, passion for botany, and deep respect for the earth's natural resources to everything she does.

RECIPE NOTES

+ Regarding portion control, Deborah Szekely reminds us that how much you eat should depend on the size and age of the container (meaning you). Recipes make 6 small or spa-sized portions (for small people) or 4 regular portions (for larger or more active people).

+ All recipes may be halved, unless otherwise noted, to serve 2 or 3 people.

+ Organic ingredients are essential. Remember that the slight premium you might pay helps support a small grower and keeps choices available to you.

+ Buy produce in season. Our seasons at the Ranch may not be the same as yours. Some climate zones get corn in late June, others must wait until August. Your local farmers' markets will be on their own schedule. If you can't find an ingredient listed in a recipe, any similar seasonal fruit or vegetable may be substituted.

+ Shop regularly at your local whole-foods co-op and your farmers' market. By supporting local growers and distributors, you vote with your dollars for better, healthier food.

+ Tofu or tempeh may be substituted for any fish or cheese in the recipes; soy milk may be substituted for dairy.

+ Low-fat or nonfat dairy products may be used in place of full-fat products such as milk or cheese, though this may change the taste and texture of the finished recipe.

+ If you are watching your sodium intake, salt may be eliminated completely from any recipe. Conversely, feel free to adjust the seasoning in any recipe to your taste.

+ Fresh herbs add a burst of incredible flavor that elevates even a simple recipe to something wonderful. So we cannot in good conscience recommend dried herbs as a substitute and urge you to buy and use fresh herbs, which are widely available all year. For the record, 1 teaspoon of whole dried herbs is roughly equivalent to 1 tablespoon of fresh herbs.

HOW TO USE THIS BOOK

This book, lovely as it is, is a tool and is meant to be used. The best cookbooks have splattered pages and sticky notes.

There's no wrong way to cook. One of our main goals is to make you feel confident in your own kitchen and with your cooking skills. Try something simple at first, and don't worry if it isn't perfect. Cooking can be as improvisational as jazz. Use your recipe as a guideline, like a melody, and go for it. Experiment. Change the recipe. Scribble notes in the margins. You'll only get better, and someday soon, like a chef, you won't really need a recipe book at all.

The La Cocina way of cooking is not about restriction and denial, but about packing more delicious "good stuff" into your daily cooking. So pile it on! Add healthy vegetables, fruit, whole grains, and legumes into your diet. Make simple changes in how (and where) you shop, what you choose, and how you cook it. This is cooking that is soul-satisfying and, as a bonus, good for you.

In some recipes, the lists of ingredients might seem long. Yes, there might seem to be much cutting and chopping. But most of those ingredients are the delicious vegetables you want to eat, and the preparation is quick and simple. Give it a try!

When you look past the recipes, you will see that this book is really about remembering how to taste. Awakening your senses will revolutionize how you look at food, how you shop, and how you cook. It's a reminder to slow down and enjoy one of life's great pleasures. And it's a plea to save real food before it's too late.

"WHEN SHALL WE LIVE,
IF NOT NOW?"
M.F.K. FISHER

The first warm touch of spring is delicious rebirth. After a long winter, the senses unfold, reawakening to light and smell. The taste of green—clean, flowering, slightly bitter, even tangy—is energizing. The garden is ready to be planted, trees suddenly shimmer with tiny leaves, and the air hums with possibilities. The earth is awake and alive—and so are we. ✴ In early May, La Cocina's floribunda roses are already blooming pink, shell white, and crimson from trellises and archways. Stands of sun-yellow marguerite daisies and a thousand Baja wildflowers wave to be noticed. By a warm stone wall, bees cling to the blue bells of borage flowers that dip and nod under their weight. Vast bushes of Jerusalem sage bloom with clusters of fuzzy yellow flowers, each holding a drop of spicy-sweet nectar in its heart. Stands of calendula, a wash of saffron and sun, line the brick pathways into the garden. Busy gardeners trundle barrow-loads of harvested greens on their way to the

SPRING
The Miracle

Ranch kitchen. The weather is clear and perfect—a wide Baja sky tossed with fat, white clouds tumbling down from mountains the color of Tecate brick. ✴ Spring has fairly exploded in the garden. Neat lines of sturdy green and white kale wave in the breeze. Delicate lettuces colored amethyst and fuchsia and lime green flutter like flags tucked between the sprawling squash vines and long rows of young tomatoes and peppers not yet in flower. By La Cocina's courtyard, hollyhocks stand as tall as cornstalks; pink-flowered sweet peas climb the fences with coiled tendrils. ✴ The earth itself seems nearly bare. Still, there's much to inspire the cook ravenous for freshness, for *green*. We crave the goodness that comes so freely from spring's first burst of growth. Later in the season, as spring slides effortlessly toward summer, come succulent berries, flowering herbs, young garlic and peas, scallions, and even a few tart early tomatoes.

Spring Dinner

✦

JICAMA SLAW WITH PINK GRAPEFRUIT

SHRIMP AND RED PEPPERS ON ROSEMARY SPRIGS

BUTTERNUT SQUASH GNOCCHI

CANDIED GINGER SORBET WITH BORAGE FLOWERS

✦

A springtime walk through the garden at Tres Estrellas, when the air is heady with flowers, inspires this menu. Awaken your taste buds with crunchy jicama slaw and succulent shrimp grilled on skewers of flowering rosemary that sparkle with lemon and fresh herbs. Transform lush tropical fruits into the world's easiest frozen dessert, and accent it with blue borage flowers.

JICAMA SLAW WITH PINK GRAPEFRUIT

❋ SERVES 6 ❋

Beneath its rough skin, jicama is pearly white, mildly sweet, and addictively juicy and crunchy, especially with a squeeze of lime. Slice it into elegant julienne and mix it with red cabbage and shredded carrots from the garden. The last of winter's limes and grapefruit sparkle in the exotic citrus-based dressing. Use this recipe to inspire seasonal variations throughout the year—Chef Jesús often substitutes cucumbers or zucchini in summer and small kohlrabis in fall. In class, he uses this recipe to teach knife technique and how to cut fine shreds (julienne).

½ SMALL JICAMA

3 MEDIUM CARROTS, PEELED

½ SMALL HEAD RED CABBAGE, CORED

¼ CUP FRESH LIME JUICE (ABOUT 2 LIMES)

1½ TABLESPOONS VEGETABLE OIL

2 TEASPOONS MINCED PEELED FRESH GINGER

1½ TABLESPOONS SMOOTH PEANUT BUTTER OR OTHER NUT BUTTER

¼ CUP COCONUT MILK

3 TABLESPOONS WATER

ZEST OF ½ LEMON (ABOUT 1 TEASPOON)

½ TEASPOON WHITE PEPPER

2 PINK GRAPEFRUITS

6 LETTUCE OR RED CABBAGE LEAVES

6 SPRIGS FRESH CILANTRO

1. With a sharp knife, mandoline, or box grater, cut the jicama, carrots, and red cabbage into fine shreds, and place in a 2-quart bowl.

2. In a blender, combine the lime juice, oil, ginger, peanut butter, coconut milk, water, lemon zest, and white pepper. Add the dressing to the shredded vegetables and toss to combine. Cover and chill.

3. Cut away all the peel and white pith from the grapefruit, then cut alongside each of the membranes to release the grapefruit segments, catching as much of the juice as you can, and add it to the slaw.

4. Serve the slaw mounded on a lettuce leaf and surrounded by a few grapefruit segments. Top the salad with a cilantro sprig.

VARIATIONS

✦ Substitute napa cabbage, bok choy, or any green that appeals to you, for jicama.

✦ Chop ¼ cup unsalted roasted peanuts and mix into the salad.

✦ Wash, stem, and chop the leaves from 6 sprigs of cilantro or 2 sprigs of basil and stir into the salad just before serving.

SHRIMP AND RED PEPPERS ON ROSEMARY SPRIGS

❋ SERVES 6 ❋

DEBORAH REMEMBERS . . . *When I was a little girl, our family lived for several years on a beach in Tahiti. We'd fish in the lagoon from our dugout outrigger canoe, and more than once I'd wake before dawn to hunt shrimp in the freshwater creek that came down from the mountains. We'd fashion torches from dead palm fronds and walk the shallows looking for deeper holes where we could scoop up shrimp trapped by the lower water level. Then at dawn we'd catch the bus into town and sell our buckets of shrimp at the local market. Of course the shrimp from the Gulf of California (Sea of Cortez) are very different from Tahitian shrimp, but I love their curled pinkness hot off the grill just the same.*

Choose slim but sturdy rosemary sprigs just strong enough to pierce the seafood, or substitute small bamboo skewers. Other herbs such as basil shine in this simple, lovely dish that brings the garden to your plate.

Cooking delicate seafood can be a tricky process. Always marinate the seafood to add flavor and moisture, cook over moderate heat, and most important, don't overcook it!

18 SPRIGS FRESH ROSEMARY (PREFERABLY IN FLOWER), ABOUT 4 INCHES LONG

18 LARGE SHRIMP

2 TABLESPOONS OLIVE OIL

1 MEDIUM SHALLOT, CHOPPED (ABOUT 1 TABLESPOON)

2 CLOVES FRESH GARLIC, PEELED AND MINCED (ABOUT 2 TEASPOONS)

1 SPRIG FRESH OREGANO, CHOPPED (ABOUT 1 TABLESPOON)

8 LARGE LEAVES FRESH BASIL, CHOPPED (ABOUT 3 TABLESPOONS)

1 SPRIG FRESH THYME LEAVES, CHOPPED (ABOUT 1 TEASPOON)

GRATED ZEST OF 1 LEMON

$1/2$ TEASPOON SEA SALT

$1/2$ TEASPOON FRESH GROUND BLACK PEPPER

1 SMALL RED BELL PEPPER, SEEDED AND CUT INTO 1-INCH SQUARES

$1 1/2$ TEASPOONS PAPRIKA

1. Strip the rosemary leaves from the sprigs, leaving one inch on top with leaves and flowers. Soak briefly in cold water.

2. Peel and devein the shrimp, leaving the tails on if you like, and pat dry. Combine the oil, shallot, garlic, herbs, lemon zest, salt, and pepper in a glass bowl. Add the shrimp and toss thoroughly with the marinade. Cover and refrigerate for at least 30 minutes.

3. Carefully thread a red pepper square onto each rosemary skewer, and follow with a shrimp. Finish with another piece of red pepper. (Use a bamboo skewer to make the holes, then slide onto the rosemary sprigs.) Sprinkle the skewers very lightly with a little paprika.

4. Preheat a gas grill or heat a grill pan over medium heat for 5 minutes. Lightly oil the cooking surface, then cook the skewers for about 3 minutes on each side, or until the shrimp are opaque but still springy to the touch.

5. Serve the shrimp on sautéed spinach with Butternut Squash Gnocchi (page 22) on the side.

VARIATION

✦ Substitute any firm fish, tempeh, or tofu for shrimp.

BUTTERNUT SQUASH GNOCCHI

❋ SERVES 10–12 ❋

Well into spring, Chef Jesús uses the hard squash that grow prolifically at Tres Estrellas—butternut squash and acorn squash are favorites. Gnocchi are easy to make and so forgiving that they are a fun team project with the non-cooks in the family. When made with squash or other orange vegetables, such as yams or sweet carrots, they take on a lovely golden color. When made with pale yellow sweet potatoes, gnocchi are cream-colored and light in texture. Any variety is delicious and can be a great way to incorporate these nutrient-rich foods into your cooking. Once you've mastered the technique, you will make them again and again.

1 ¾ POUNDS BUTTERNUT SQUASH

3 EGG YOLKS

1 TEASPOON KOSHER SALT

½ TEASPOON FRESH GROUND BLACK PEPPER

¼ TEASPOON FRESH GRATED NUTMEG

2 TO 2½ CUPS SIFTED ALL-PURPOSE FLOUR, PLUS MORE AS NEEDED

2 TABLESPOONS OLIVE OIL

SALT AND FRESH GROUND BLACK PEPPER TO TASTE

1. Preheat the oven to 350 degrees F.

2. Cut the squash in half and scoop out the seeds. Wrap in foil and bake the squash for about 1 hour, or until very soft.

3. When the squash has cooled just enough to be handled comfortably, scoop out the flesh and either run through the finest disk of a food mill or force through the holes of a strainer into a bowl (to remove any fiber).

4. Add the egg yolks, salt, pepper, and nutmeg and beat well by hand to combine. Stir in the flour a half-cup at a time. The drier the squash, the less flour you will need, and the lighter the gnocchi will be.

5. When the dough becomes too stiff to stir easily, turn it out onto a well-floured board. Use your hands to work in any remaining flour a little at a time, until the dough holds its shape but is still very soft.

6. Fill a wide, deep saucepan with at least 3 inches of water. Add a heaping tablespoon of kosher salt and bring the water to a gentle simmer. (Don't let the water come to a rolling boil.)

7. Divide the dough into 12 equal pieces. On a floured board, shape each portion into a rope the thickness of your thumb and cut into 1-inch pieces.

8. Lift the pieces from the board with a thin spatula. With your fingers, gently reshape the gnocchi into cylinders and drop them into the simmering water.

9. The gnocchi will sink to the bottom and seem to stick. Don't touch them. In a minute or so, they will release and bob to the surface. After another few seconds, the gnocchi will roll over. Cook for 2 minutes. When they are firm and plump, remove them with a slotted spoon and set on a lightly oiled tray.

10. When all the gnocchi are cooked, wrap and chill them until you are ready for the final cooking. (They may also be frozen at this point.)

11. To serve, bring a pot of salted water to a boil. Drop the gnocchi into the boiling water and cook for 1 minute, then scoop out with a skimmer or slotted spoon.

12. Heat the oil in a large nonstick sauté pan. Sauté the gnocchi in batches until they are lightly browned on both sides. Season with salt and pepper and serve hot.

CANDIED GINGER SORBET
WITH BORAGE FLOWERS

❋ SERVES 6 ❋

Borage grows in silvery heaps under the windows of Tres Estrellas' old kitchen. The delicate deep-blue flower bells that sway in every breeze taste faintly and pleasantly of cucumbers. They look beautiful on the sorbet and bring a little of the garden inside. Any sweet edible flower or flowering herb may be used instead.

Jesús uses this recipe often, making slight changes based on availability. At the market, use your nose to choose the best fruit. If it smells sweet and wonderful, it's at its height of flavor.

1 ½ BANANAS (ABOUT 1 CUP), CHOPPED INTO 1-INCH CUBES

2 CUPS RIPE BERRIES, MANGO, PAPAYA, KIWI, PINEAPPLE, OR OTHER FRUIT, PEELED AND CUT INTO 1-INCH PIECES

½ CUP FRESH ORANGE JUICE

2 TABLESPOONS FRESH LIME JUICE (ABOUT 1 LIME)

ZEST OF 1 LIME

2 TO 3 TABLESPOONS MINCED CANDIED GINGER, OR MORE TO TASTE

BLUE BORAGE FLOWERS OR OTHER SWEET HERB FLOWERS, SUCH AS LAVENDER

1. Freeze fruit cubes on a sheet pan for several hours until they are solid. Remove from freezer and let stand about 5 minutes.

2. Place the fruit in the bowl of a food processor with the orange and lime juice, the lime zest, and ginger. Puree until creamy.

3. Add ginger, as needed, to taste. Serve in chilled sorbet dishes, martini glasses, or bowls. Garnish each serving with a few flowers.

VARIATIONS

✦ Substitute other seasonal fruit as available, but keep the banana—it lends a creamy texture to the sorbet.

✦ Substitute up to 1 tablespoon finely grated peeled fresh ginger for the candied ginger.

Tres Estrellas Brunch

✦

TUSCAN FARRO SALAD

TRES ESTRELLAS FRITTATA
WITH ZUCCHINI FLOWERS AND GOAT CHEESE

ORANGE SAFFRON PINE-NUT BREAD

RICOTTA CHEESECAKE WITH BERRIES AND LAVENDER

✦

*The legendary frittata served to guests after the breakfast hike to Tres Estrellas is
the center of an easy brunch to share with friends. A deliciously unusual farro salad
full of crunchy vegetables and Jesús' fabulous Orange Saffron Pine-Nut Bread round
out the main course. Dessert is citrus cheesecake, pretty as a centerpiece with
lots of agave-sweetened berries and a spike of fragrant lavender flowers.*

TUSCAN FARRO SALAD

※ SERVES 6 ※

Farro was once the food staple of the ancient Romans. Its plump grains are deliciously nutty and chewy. Farro is higher in B vitamins than many types of wheat and may even be tolerated by some wheat-sensitive diners. Jesús loves the texture and flavor of farro, but barley or wild rice are good substitutes (see Basics, page 166, for more on unusual grains.) Raw cauliflower and broccoli, broken into tiny pieces, add great flavor and a nutritional boost. Salvador grows bright purple and yellow cauliflowers that add amazing color to salads. The deliciously crunchy, vividly colored salad tastes best at room temperature on a bed of lettuce.

2 CUPS BASIC VEGETABLE STOCK (PAGE 176) OR WATER

1 CUP FARRO

1 RED BELL PEPPER, CUT INTO 1/4-INCH DICE

1 1/2 CELERY STALKS, CUT INTO 1/4-INCH DICE

2 GREEN ONIONS, TRIMMED AND FINELY SLICED

12 FRESH BASIL LEAVES, CHOPPED

1/2 CUP SUN-DRIED TOMATOES, CUT INTO 1/2-INCH PIECES (SEE NOTE)

1/4 CUP FRESH FLAT-LEAF PARSLEY LEAVES, CHOPPED

1/4 CUP CHOPPED CASHEWS, SUNFLOWER SEEDS, OR PINE NUTS

3 TABLESPOONS FRESH LIME OR LEMON JUICE, OR TO TASTE

2 TABLESPOONS EXTRA-VIRGIN OLIVE OIL

1/2 TEASPOON SALT

1/8 TEASPOON FRESH GRATED NUTMEG

BUTTER, LIMESTONE, OR RED LETTUCE LEAVES, OR 6 CUPS MIXED GREENS

6 SPRIGS FRESH CILANTRO OR FLAT-LEAF PARSLEY (OPTIONAL)

1. In a small stockpot, bring stock or water to a boil over medium-high heat. Add the farro and stir. Return to boil. Reduce heat to low, cover, and simmer for 35 minutes, or until grain is tender. Drain off any excess water, stir, and cool until the grains are no longer steaming.

2. In a large bowl, combine the farro and the next 11 ingredients.

3. Line 6 salad plates with lettuce or 1 cup of mixed greens, and spoon 1/2 cup of the salad onto the greens. Garnish with cilantro or flat-leaf parsley, if desired.

NOTE: If the sun-dried tomatoes are hard or brittle, soak for 30 minutes in hot water to soften.

VARIATIONS

✦ Add 1/2 cup cooked green peas or edamame (green soybeans).

✦ Serve with Basil Balsamic Dressing (page 79) on the side.

TRES ESTRELLAS FRITTATA WITH ZUCCHINI FLOWERS AND GOAT CHEESE

❋ SERVES 6 ❋

Guests hike two miles from the Ranch to Tres Estrellas at dawn just to enjoy this delicious frittata before the garden tour. It's like tasting the whole garden in a single bite (without the dirt, of course). Not surprisingly, this is one of the Ranch's most requested recipes, and it can be doubled or tripled to feed a larger group.

Use any seasonal vegetables that catch your eye (chopped fresh tomatoes are a frequent addition in summer) and always include some kind of dark leafy green. The same sautéed vegetables used in this frittata also make a great filling for empanadas, quesadillas, or crepes.

In late spring, a handful of delicate zucchini flowers (*flor de calabasa*) adds an authentically Mexican taste. Sometimes Jesús sautés the zucchini flowers and puts them on top, or simply uses the whole flower as a garnish.

1 TABLESPOON OLIVE OIL

1/2 ONION, PEELED AND CUT INTO 3/8-INCH DICE

1 CLOVE GARLIC, PEELED AND MINCED

1/2 JALAPEÑO, SEEDED AND MINCED (OPTIONAL)

2 CUPS MIXED VEGETABLES (SUCH AS CAULIFLOWER, BROCCOLI, CARROTS, SQUASH, LEEKS, ZUCCHINI, CABBAGE, KOHLRABI, RAPINI, AND POTATOES), CUT INTO 1/2-INCH PIECES

2 CUPS LEAFY GREENS (SUCH AS SPINACH, CHARD, COLLARD, KALE, AND NETTLE) STEMMED AND CUT INTO 1-INCH PIECES

1 GREEN, RED, OR YELLOW BELL PEPPER, SEEDED AND CUT INTO 1/2-INCH PIECES

2 MEDIUM TOMATOES, CORED, SEEDED AND CUT INTO 1/4-INCH PIECES

6 ZUCCHINI FLOWERS, RINSED, DRAINED, AND CUT INTO 1-INCH PIECES

1 TEASPOON GROUND CUMIN

1 TEASPOON SEA SALT

6 EXTRA-LARGE EGGS, BEATEN

2 TABLESPOONS CHOPPED MIXED FRESH HERBS (SUCH AS PARSLEY, BASIL, THYME, AND OREGANO)

2 OUNCES GOAT CHEESE, FETA, ASIAGO, OR PARMESAN, CRUMBLED

TRES ESTRELLAS SALSA (RECIPE FOLLOWS)

1. Preheat the oven to 350 degrees F.

2. In a 10-inch ovenproof sauté pan, heat the oil over medium-high heat for 1 minute. Add the onion, garlic, and jalapeño and cook for 2 minutes, stirring constantly, until just softened.

3. Add the mixed vegetables, greens, and bell pepper. Cook for 10 minutes, stirring occasionally, until barely tender. Stir in the tomatoes, zucchini flowers, cumin, and 1/2 teaspoon of the salt. Remove the pan from the heat.

4. Combine the eggs with the remaining 1/2 teaspoon of salt. Stir in the chopped herbs and pour the eggs over the vegetables. Stir to combine. Sprinkle the cheese evenly over the top.

5. Bake for about 20 to 25 minutes, or until the eggs are firm and the top of the frittata is puffed and lightly browned. Serve on warmed plates or directly from the pan for buffet presentation with the salsa of your choice.

VARIATION

✦ Make a sauce of plain yogurt mixed with plenty of chopped fresh dill and a touch of fresh lemon juice to serve with or instead of the salsa.

TRES ESTRELLAS SALSA

❋ MAKES ABOUT 2 CUPS ❋

This is a typical cooked salsa, using *guajillo* chiles. These mild dried chiles have a wonderful, rich flavor that will remind you of enchilada sauce. Dried California chiles may be substituted for the *guajillos*. See "About Dried Chiles," page 40, for more information about buying and handling dried chiles.

2 DRIED *GUAJILLO* CHILES

1 DRIED HOT CHILE, SUCH AS CHILE DE ARBOL (OPTIONAL)

1/2 CUP HOT WATER

2 ROMA TOMATOES

1 CLOVE GARLIC, NOT PEELED

1/2 TEASPOON SEA SALT

1/4 CUP FRESH CILANTRO LEAVES, CHOPPED

1. Set a heavy-bottomed sauté pan over medium-high heat. When the pan is very hot, press the dried chiles onto the hot surface with a spatula for a few seconds on each side, being careful not to burn or scorch them. Remove the chiles from the pan, cool, and remove stems and seeds. Break the chiles into pieces and place in a blender jar with the hot water. Soak for 30 minutes.

2. Lay a sheet of aluminum foil in the same pan and pan-roast the tomatoes until well-blackened on all sides. Add the tomatoes to the blender. Pan-roast the garlic clove in its skin, turning often, until it is soft. Peel and add to the blender, along with the salt.

3. Puree the salsa until it is smooth, and stir in the cilantro. Thin the sauce, if necessary, with a little water.

NOTE: While *guajillos* are generally not spicy, be careful to specify mild *guajillos* (*guajillo no pico*, in Spanish) when you buy them.

ORANGE SAFFRON PINE-NUT BREAD

❋ MAKES 2 LOAVES ❋

This delicious bread is richer than Rancho La Puerta Flaxseed Bread (page 114), but easy to make even if you have never made bread before, and it freezes beautifully so you can keep it on hand. You may substitute whole-wheat flour for some or all of the all-purpose flour—the bread will be a little heavier.

1 TEASPOON SPANISH SAFFRON THREADS

4 CUPS WARM WATER

2 TABLESPOONS ACTIVE DRY YEAST

1 CUP AGAVE SYRUP OR MAPLE SYRUP

ZEST OF 2 LARGE ORANGES

½ CUP (1 STICK) UNSALTED BUTTER, MELTED

1 TABLESPOON SEA SALT

4 CUPS WHOLE-WHEAT FLOUR

1 CUP TOASTED PINE NUTS

4 TO 5 CUPS UNBLEACHED ALL-PURPOSE FLOUR, PLUS MORE AS NEEDED

1. Soak the saffron threads in ½ cup of the water for 30 minutes.

2. Combine the remaining 3 ½ cups of water and the yeast. Let stand until frothy, about 10 minutes.

3. Stir the syrup, orange zest, saffron, melted butter, and salt into the yeast until thoroughly combined. Add the wheat flour and mix until smooth.

4. Stir in the pine nuts and most of the all-purpose flour, reserving 1 cup. The dough should be a little sticky. Flour the countertop with some of the remaining flour and knead the dough until it is smooth and elastic, about 5 minutes, adding flour to the surface as needed to make the dough manageable. You may not use all the flour, or you may need a little more. The final dough should feel moist and a little tacky, but not sticky or wet.

5. Place the dough in a clean, lightly oiled bowl. Turn over once to coat, and cover with a barely damp tea towel to prevent the dough from drying out. Let the dough rise in a warm, draft-free place until it has doubled in bulk, about 2 hours.

6. Punch down the dough. Divide into 2 equal portions. Spread or roll each portion into a rectangle and pinch the edges together.

7. Place each loaf in an oiled loaf pan. Cover and let rise in a warm, draft-free place until the loaves have doubled in bulk, about 40 minutes.

8. Bake in a preheated 375-degree F oven for one hour, or until the tops are browned and the loaves sound hollow when tapped. Cool completely on a rack before slicing.

AGAVE SYRUP

Agave syrup is used at the Ranch as an all-purpose sweetener as well as for baking and for caramelizing nuts. As its name implies, agave syrup is made by tapping the desert agave plant (the same one used to make tequila) for sap in the same way that maple sap is harvested. The thin syrup, available in clear or amber colors, is lightly sweet, and it may be used interchangeably with honey or maple syrup.

RICOTTA CHEESECAKE
WITH BERRIES AND LAVENDER

❋ SERVES 6 ❋

DEBORAH REMEMBERS . . . *One of my mother's beliefs was that her children should not drink milk or eat dairy products, but on birthdays and holidays Mom made a big exception, and we ate cheesecake. It's been one of my passions ever since. In the early years at the Ranch, I experimented with making cheesecake using goat's milk (we had our own herd of ninety goats roaming the slopes of Mount Kuchumaa), but it just wasn't the same as the sweet, creamy wedge I had enjoyed as a little girl. This cheesecake, with its zesty orange and berry flavors, is fantastic.*

To the east of La Cocina is the original garden site, abandoned a number of years ago, where today Tres Estrellas' flock of chickens stays busy catching bugs and blackberry brambles grow wild under the sycamores. The ripe blackberries are soft and tart, but so full of flavor that you can't stop eating them. The best ones are always deep inside the brambles, past a gauntlet of thorns—and they are worth every scratch.

The ricotta-based cheesecake is perfect with any kind of ripe berry, lightly drizzled with agave syrup. Scatter a few lavender blossoms or other edible flower petals over the cheesecake to add a beautiful, sweet floral touch.

3 CUPS CORN OR WHEAT FLAKE CEREAL

1 CUP AGAVE OR MAPLE SYRUP

3 EGG WHITES

2 WHOLE EGGS

2 CUPS RICOTTA OR COTTAGE CHEESE

8 OUNCES CREAM CHEESE

½ CUP SOUR CREAM

2 TEASPOONS VANILLA EXTRACT

ZEST OF 1 ORANGE

2 CUPS RIPE SEASONAL BERRIES (SUCH AS BLACKBERRIES, RASPBERRIES, BLUEBERRIES, OR STRAWBERRIES)

LAVENDER BLOSSOMS, ROSE PETALS, OR OTHER EDIBLE FLOWERS (OPTIONAL)

1. Preheat the oven to 325 degrees F.

2. In the bowl of food processor, combine the cereal and ¼ cup of the syrup, pulsing until coarsely ground. Press the crumbs firmly into the bottom of an oiled 9-inch springform pan or a cake pan with a removable bottom.

3. Cut a piece of parchment paper to line the sides of the pan, fit the paper snugly around the inside edge, and brush the paper lightly with oil. (This will make it easier to release the cheesecake from the pan.)

4. In a clean bowl of a food processor or in a blender, combine the egg whites, whole eggs, ricotta or cottage cheese, cream cheese, sour cream, vanilla, orange zest, and ½ cup of the syrup. Process until completely smooth, then pour the cheese mixture over the crust.

5. Bake for 1 hour, or until a toothpick inserted in the center comes out clean. Cool on a rack for 30 minutes, then release the cheesecake and remove the paper. Chill, uncovered for several hours, until completely firm.

6. To serve, set the cake on a serving plate and top with the berries. Drizzle the remaining ¼ cup syrup over the fruit and decorate with lavender blossoms, rose petals, or other edible flowers, if desired.

Hacienda

✦

AGUAS FRESCAS

MEXICAN COLESLAW WITH RED AND GREEN CABBAGE,
JICAMA, AND CILANTRO VINAIGRETTE

LASAGNA AZTECA WITH SPINACH AND ANCHO CHILE SALSA

CREAMY DARK CHOCOLATE FLAN WITH FRESH BERRIES

✦

*Rancho La Puerta's deep Mexican roots inspired this menu, which features
Lasagna Azteca, one of the Ranch's oldest and most beloved recipes. In Mexico,
a dish like this is called a* pastel *and is a casserole of corn tortillas and vegetables,
layered with a richly authentic sauce of mild ancho chiles. The light coleslaw,
made from red and green cabbages from the garden, borrows its colors from the
Mexican flag and has a distinctive cilantro flavor. The chocolate flan may be
served warm from the oven or chilled and garnished with fresh berries.*

AGUAS FRESCAS

In Mexico, healthful fruit-based *aguas* are preferred to sugary sodas. Every class at La Cocina begins with one of these unique drinks, served in thick blue-rimmed glasses. Serve your *aguas* over ice in short tumblers. Note that except for the Lime Agua Fresca, the sweetener is always optional—be sure to taste before adding.

Any fruit can be made into a delicious *agua fresca*: mango, papaya, pineapple, guava, or pink grapefruit. For best flavor, use fresh-squeezed juices. Freeze *aguas frescas* in ice cube trays and use instead of plain ice cubes for a burst of color and flavor that won't dilute your drink. Add chopped mint or experiment with basil or lavender. Garnish with sliced fruit, flowers or cucumber sticks. Some flavor ideas to get you started are cranberry-lime, lemon with grenadine syrup, mango-lime, peach and berry, and strawberry with balsamic vinegar.

CUCUMBER MINT AGUA FRESCA

❋ MAKES 8 CUPS ❋

This refreshingly different beverage is sure to become a favorite. Jesús sometimes purees a bit of fresh fennel with the cucumbers. Garnish, if you like, with a cucumber stick or a few mint leaves.

2 LARGE CUCUMBERS (ABOUT 1½ POUNDS), PEELED AND CUT INTO LARGE PIECES

4 CUPS FRESH ULFILTERED APPLE JUICE

1 CUP FRESH LIME JUICE

1 CUP MINT LEAVES

6 TABLESPOONS AGAVE SYRUP (OPTIONAL)

In a blender, puree the first 4 ingredients until smooth. Taste and add some or all of the syrup if you prefer a sweeter flavor.

LIME AGUA FRESCA

❋ MAKES 6 CUPS ❋

This recipe offers a twist on a traditional favorite. Try it using fresh lemon juice and mint, or a combination of lime and orange. Garnish with a citrus slice in a contrasting color and a sprig of cilantro.

5 CUPS WATER

¾ CUP LIME JUICE

½ CUP AGAVE SYRUP, OR TO TASTE

2 TABLESPOONS FINELY CHOPPED CILANTRO (OPTIONAL)

Place all of the ingredients in a blender and blend well. Taste and add more syrup, if needed.

WATERMELON AGUA FRESCA

❋ MAKES 8 CUPS ❋

Bright pink and naturally sweet, watermelon (*sandia*) *agua fresca* is hands-down the favorite in Mexico. The raspberries are an unusual addition. Garnish with a sprig of purple basil or a lavender flower.

1½ POUNDS SEEDLESS WATERMELON, RIND REMOVED, CUT INTO 1-INCH CHUNKS

1½ CUPS FROZEN RASPBERRIES

1 CUP FRESH UNFILTERED APPLE JUICE

3 TABLESPOONS AGAVE SYRUP (OPTIONAL)

In a food processor, puree the first 3 ingredients until smooth (you may need to do this in batches). Taste and add some or all of the syrup if you prefer a sweeter flavor.

APPLE AGUA FRESCA

❋ MAKES 6 CUPS ❋

This *agua fresca* has a bright, refreshing flavor. Garnish with thin slices of apple. For a less pulpy drink, peel the apples.

3 MEDIUM GREEN APPLES, PEELS ON, CORED AND CHOPPED

2 CUPS WATER

1 CUP APPLE JUICE

JUICE OF 3 LIMES

2 TABLESPOONS CHOPPED FRESH MINT

2 TABLESPOONS AGAVE SYRUP (OPTIONAL)

In a blender, puree the first 5 ingredients until smooth. Taste and add some or all of the syrup if you prefer a sweeter flavor.

PALETAS

Paletas are Mexican popsicles—simply frozen fruit juice on a stick. Make yours from any of the *agua fresca* recipes here or puree fresh fruit with a little water, pour into molds, and freeze. Sweetener is optional. Use a single fruit or combine juices to create something new and intriguing. Try some of the exotic fruit juices sold in Asian and Latin markets. A squeeze of lime accentuates the sweetness of ripe fruit. Flavor as you would any *agua fresca*, with fresh mint or other herbs. Molds and sticks for *paletas* can be purchased at cookware stores.

MEXICAN COLESLAW
WITH RED AND GREEN CABBAGE, JICAMA, AND CILANTRO VINAIGRETTE

✳ SERVES 6 ✳

The sturdy cabbage, with its flamboyant flourish of leaves, grows prolifically most of the year. Mexican cooks love both cabbage and radishes and use them in everything from taco garnishes to soups. This salad gets a little zing from the radish, so the jalapeño in the dressing is, as always, optional. The light cilantro dressing would be good on any salad.

3 CUPS SHREDDED RED CABBAGE

3 CUPS SHREDDED NAPA OR GREEN CABBAGE

1 BUNCH RADISHES, THINLY SLICED

1/2 SMALL JICAMA (ABOUT 1 1/2 CUPS), PEELED AND CUT INTO SMALL CUBES

2 GREEN ONIONS, TRIMMED AND THINLY SLICED

CILANTRO DRESSING

4 TABLESPOONS FRESH LIME JUICE

4 TABLESPOONS RICE VINEGAR

3/4 CUP PLAIN YOGURT

1 TEASPOON SEA SALT

3 TABLESPOONS EXTRA-VIRGIN OLIVE OIL

1 CUP FRESH CILANTRO LEAVES, CHOPPED

1 JALAPEÑO, SEEDED AND MINCED (OPTIONAL)

1. In a bowl, toss together the cabbage, radishes, jicama, and onions.

2. In a blender, puree the lime juice, vinegar, yogurt, salt, and oil. Stir in the cilantro and jalapeño, pour over the vegetables, and toss to combine. Cover and refrigerate for at least 1 hour before serving.

VARIATIONS

✦ Top the salad with toasted sunflower or pumpkin seeds and bits of fresh orange segments.

✦ Jesús suggests adding grated carrots, cucumber, or small kohlrabi to the salad.

✦ For a vegan dressing, replace the yogurt with an equal amount of soy yogurt or silken tofu.

LOCAL, SUSTAINABLE, ORGANIC

Our supermarkets overflow with food imported from all over the world. This is indicative of our national wealth—we can have whatever we want whenever we want it—but it is also a kind of invisible poverty. Generally speaking, food raised close to where you live is better all around—the fresher the produce, the more nutrients it contains and the better it tastes. But locally raised food is almost never sold in local supermarkets. Imported produce is cheaper, and processed foods have higher profit margins and a longer shelf life than fresh.

The importation of foodstuffs is a Pandora's box of problems. There is little government oversight, and what regulation exists is under constant assault by agribusiness and grocers who want standards weakened, not strengthened. We urge you to buy organic foods whenever possible. They are better for you and better for the planet. Many pesticides and herbicides banned for use in the United States are used on food grown elsewhere for export, exposing not only those farm workers but also produce–buying Americans to potentially dangerous chemicals that end up right back on the food we buy. In foreign countries, food grown for export pushes out crops that could be eaten by locals.

Importing cheap foods also undermines local producers and forces small farmers from their land. Monoculture and standardized crops are reducing genetic diversity and choice, while genetically altered crops are sifting out all over the world with unknown results. Sustainable farming practices will give small farmers a shot at survival, and that means real choices about what to eat and where it comes from.

Last, but certainly not least, enormous amounts of energy are burned up flying and shipping out-of-season foods around the globe. Do you really need fresh raspberries in December?

LASAGNA AZTECA WITH SPINACH AND ANCHO CHILE SALSA

❊ SERVES 6–8 GENEROUSLY ❊

DEBORAH REMEMBERS . . . *Within the first week of arriving at the Ranch, we discovered the delicious corn tortillas that were made in town, served warm and wrapped in a plain newsprintlike paper. Eventually we discovered their other possibilities when layered with cheese, vegetables, and a savory sauce made with dried chiles into this delicious "lasagna"—a Ranch favorite for decades.*

What makes this lasagna Azteca is the use of corn. Mexico is the cradle of the world's corn, and corn is still a staple food today, much as it has been for thousands of years. Substitute any other seasonal vegetables from the market for those listed here. You can make the lasagna a day ahead and bake it just before serving. The recipe may be doubled, so make extra and freeze it for another meal.

2 TABLESPOONS EXTRA-VIRGIN OLIVE OIL

1 WHITE ONION, CUT INTO ¼-INCH DICE (ABOUT 2 CUPS)

1 CUP CORN KERNELS

6 CLOVES GARLIC, PEELED AND MINCED

1 YELLOW OR GREEN ZUCCHINI, CUT INTO ¼-INCH DICE

1 RED BELL PEPPER, SEEDED AND CUT INTO ¼-INCH DICE

11 OUNCES OYSTER MUSHROOMS, SLICED (ABOUT 5 CUPS)

1 TEASPOON SALT

6 OUNCES SPINACH, STEMS REMOVED (ABOUT 4 CUPS)

3 WHOLE EGGS

¼ CUP CRUMBLED COTIJA OR FETA CHEESE (SEE NOTE)

1 CUP GRATED MOZZARELLA CHEESE

2 CUPS RICOTTA CHEESE

½ CUP FRESH BASIL, CHOPPED

1 SMALL BUNCH FRESH CILANTRO, WASHED AND CHOPPED (ABOUT ½ CUP)

10 CORN TORTILLAS

ANCHO CHILE SALSA (RECIPE FOLLOWS)

1. Preheat the oven to 350 degrees F.

2. In a large sauté pan, heat the olive oil over medium heat. Add the onion and sauté until the onions are soft and translucent, about 5 minutes. Add the corn, garlic, zucchini, bell pepper, and mushrooms, and cook for 3 minutes, until the vegetables soften.

3. Season with ½ teaspoon of salt, then add the spinach. Continue cooking until the spinach is wilted. Remove from the heat and set aside.

4. In the bowl of a food processor or in a blender, combine the eggs, cotija, mozzarella, and ricotta. Add the remaining ½ teaspoon of salt and process until smooth. Stir in the basil and cilantro.

5. Spray an 11 × 8-inch baking dish with olive oil. Dip 5 tortillas in the salsa and lay them across the bottom of the pan. Spread the cheese evenly over the tortillas, then the sautéed vegetables over the cheese, and place the remaining tortillas on top. Pour 1 cup of salsa over the top.

6. Bake for 50 to 60 minutes, or until the cheese mixture is firm. Remove the lasagna from the oven and let it cool 10 minutes. Cut into squares and serve with the remaining salsa on the side.

NOTE: Cotija is a crumbly, salty cheese similar to a dry feta. It is used in small quantities to add richness and savor to salads, soups, and cooked beans.

ANCHO CHILE SALSA

This mellow salsa is made with ancho chiles, which are dried poblano chiles. The chiles are prepared (see page 40) and cooked with tomatoes and tart tomatillos. This is a good all-around salsa that will enhance the flavor of almost any dish. A rich tomato flavor is important in this salsa, so when tomatoes are out of season, Jesús will often substitute good-quality canned organic tomatoes.

2 TEASPOONS OLIVE OIL

1/2 MEDIUM ONION, CUT INTO 1/2-INCH DICE

3 SMALL GARLIC CLOVES, PEELED AND CHOPPED

2 DRIED ANCHO CHILES, SEEDED AND TORN INTO PIECES

3 DRIED *GUAJILLO* OR CALIFORNIA CHILES, SEEDED AND TORN INTO PIECES

2 ROMA TOMATOES, CORED, SEEDED, AND ROUGHLY CHOPPED

4 LARGE GREEN TOMATILLOS, HUSKS REMOVED, WASHED, AND ROUGHLY CHOPPED

2 CUPS WATER OR BASIC VEGETABLE STOCK (PAGE 176)

1 TEASPOON SEA SALT, PLUS MORE TO TASTE

1/4 TEASPOON FRESH GROUND PEPPER

2 TABLESPOONS FRESH MEXICAN OREGANO, OR 1 TABLESPOON DRIED (SEE NOTE)

FRESH CILANTRO (12 SPRIGS), ABOUT 1/2 CUP, STEMMED AND CHOPPED

1. In a 10-inch sauté pan, heat the oil over medium heat. Add the onion, garlic, and dried chiles, and cook, stirring often, for about 5 minutes, or until the onions are soft and you can smell the chiles.

2. Add the tomatoes and tomatillos, reduce the heat slightly, and cook for another 10 minutes, stirring often.

3. Add the water or stock, 1 teaspoon of salt, and pepper. Bring to a simmer over high heat, then reduce the heat to medium-low and cook for 20 minutes.

4. Stir in the oregano, cool for a few minutes, puree the sauce in a blender until smooth, then stir in the cilantro.

NOTE: Be sure to use Mexican oregano, which has a milder taste than Mediterranean varieties.

ABOUT DRIED CHILES

Dried chiles are essential to Mexican cooking, adding color and complex flavor for which there is no substitute. Buy dried chiles in small quantities. They keep for months in the freezer, well-wrapped. They should be flexible and clean-looking, never broken or dusty. Dried chiles must be cooked to bring out their unique flavors, which can range from grassy to raisin-sweet, tobacco to herbal, mild to fiery hot. Most dry chiles are not spicy, though heat is always unpredictable from one chile to the next. Any spiciness will be concentrated in the ribs and seeds, so generally speaking, smaller chiles and those with more ribs and seeds are spicier.

There are two ways to prepare dried chiles. Whichever method you use, always wear gloves, work in a well-ventilated area, and wash your knife and cutting board immediately after use.

✦ If you are making a pureed salsa, like Ancho Chile Salsa (page 39), remove the stems, seeds, and ribs from the chiles. Tear into pieces and sauté in oil. Some recipes will also add onions and garlic at this point. Add water or stock and any other ingredients, such as tomato, that the recipe calls for. Cook until soft, then puree.

✦ To make a puree of chiles to add to something else, such as a soup, heat a dry frying pan (cast iron is ideal) over medium-high heat. Press the chiles flat against the hot pan with a spatula, cook only for a few seconds on each side, until the chiles are fragrant and soft. Be careful not to scorch or burn them. Remove the stems, seeds, and ribs. (If a recipe calls for ground chiles, toasted cleaned chiles may be ground to a powder at this point.) Tear the chiles into small pieces and soak in enough hot water to cover until soft. Drain the chiles and puree.

COMMONLY USED DRIED CHILES

ANCHO	Dried poblano chiles. They have a mild flavor with little or no heat.
PASILLA	Often mislabeled as anchos. They are wrinkled (*pasilla* means "little raisin"), and have a sweeter flavor.
MULATO	Nearly black in color. Their flavor is complex and herbal rather than sweet. They are earthier and more pungent than anchos.
GUAJILLO	Long, slim, smooth, and dark reddish. California and New Mexico chiles are similar but milder.
CHIPOTLE	Dried, smoked, red jalapeños with a smoky and spicy-sweet flavor. They are sold dried or in small cans in tomato sauce and vinegar (adobo).

CREAMY DARK CHOCOLATE FLAN
WITH FRESH BERRIES

❋ SERVES 10 ❋

This simple flan may be made a day ahead and served chilled, or popped in the oven while the rest of the meal is prepared, and enjoyed warm. Either way, serve with ripe juicy berries, locally grown. Little old-fashioned strawberries are soft and sweet as honey when in season, and they put imported berries to shame. Jesús encourages students to freeze organic berries while they are at their peak and use them during fall and winter instead of buying imported berries out of season, or use any ripe seasonal fruit. Use good-quality semisweet chips or chopped block chocolate. Avoid baking chips, which are specifically for use in cookies.

2½ CUPS MILK

1 CUP (6 OUNCES) SEMISWEET CHOCOLATE CHIPS

2 WHOLE LARGE EGGS, AT ROOM TEMPERATURE

3 LARGE EGG YOLKS, AT ROOM TEMPERATURE (SEE NOTE)

2 TABLESPOONS PURE VANILLA EXTRACT

½ CUP DARK MAPLE OR DARK AGAVE SYRUP

FRESH BERRIES FOR GARNISH

1. Preheat the oven to 350 degrees F.

2. In a small saucepan, heat the milk over medium-low heat but do not boil. Remove from the heat and stir in the chocolate until melted.

3. In a blender, combine the whole eggs, egg yolks, vanilla, and syrup. Add a small amount of the warm chocolate mixture and blend briefly. With the blender still running, add the rest of the chocolate in a steady stream.

4. Pour the mixture into 10 lightly oiled 6-ounce ramekins or custard cups, filling to within ¼ inch of the rim.

5. Place the ramekins in a rectangular baking pan with high sides, and carefully pour 1 inch of boiling water into the pan. Cover with foil and bake on the middle rack of the oven for 50 minutes to 1 hour, or until the custards are no longer jiggly in the centers. Remove from the oven and take off the foil.

6. Serve the custards warm from the oven in their dishes, or chilled and unmolded onto small plates. Garnish with seasonal berries, such as strawberries or blackberries.

NOTE: Put leftover egg whites to good use in omelets and baked goods, or in Ranch Chiles Rellenos with Ancho Chile Salsa (page 124).

VARIATION
✦ To reduce the fat in this recipe, substitute 2 egg whites for the 3 egg yolks.

Company's Coming

✦

YOUNG GARLIC SOUP WITH WILD MUSHROOMS

MIXED SEAFOOD STEAMED IN PARCHMENT
WITH SHALLOTS AND WHITE WINE

PESTO LINGUINE WITH LEMON ZEST, SUN-DRIED TOMATO, AND SNOW PEAS

AVOCADO SORBET IN PAPAYA WITH AGED BALSAMIC VINEGAR

✦

This menu celebrates the ephemeral nature of spring—the brief, delightful fling of peas, a perfumed broth of young garlic and earthy mushrooms, bright green pesto slithering over hot lemon-scented pasta, aromatic steam from a puffed packet of seafood laced with herbs and shallots, and avocado that melts on the tongue. Because the dishes are so quick, timing is important. Serve the seafood first to allow each person to open their packet. Pass the pasta, freshly tossed with pesto and grated lemon zest. Then transfer the seafood and its juices onto the pasta. These flavors together are really something special.

YOUNG GARLIC SOUP
WITH WILD MUSHROOMS

❋ SERVES 6 ❋

The infant garlic bulb carries just a whisper of its future pungency. It has a short season, and Jesús uses it in all his savory recipes while he can get it. Here, the tender, creamy bulb is infused into an earthy broth of leeks, dried shiitake mushrooms, and fresh mushrooms, with just a hint of fresh ginger. The surprise finish of chopped celery leaves is fresh and unique.

5 WHOLE DRIED SHIITAKE OR OTHER DRIED MUSHROOMS (ABOUT ½ OUNCE)

1 CUP HOT WATER OR BASIC VEGETABLE STOCK (PAGE 176)

2 TEASPOONS OLIVE OIL

¼ CUP FINELY CHOPPED CELERY

¼ CUP FINELY CHOPPED SHALLOT OR WHITE ONION

¼ CUP FINELY MINCED YOUNG GARLIC

1 LEEK, WHITE PART ONLY, FINELY CHOPPED

4 OUNCES OYSTER MUSHROOMS, CHOPPED (ABOUT 1¼ CUPS)

4 OUNCES BUTTON OR CREMINI MUSHROOMS, CHOPPED (ABOUT 1¼ CUPS)

1 TEASPOON MINCED, PEELED, FRESH GINGER

3 CUPS WATER OR BASIC VEGETABLE STOCK (PAGE 176)

1 TO 2 TABLESPOONS ORGANIC WHITE MISO PASTE, OR TO TASTE (OPTIONAL)

2 TABLESPOONS CHOPPED YOUNG GARLIC STEMS OR CHIVES

1 TABLESPOON CHOPPED CELERY LEAVES OR FRESH FLAT-LEAF PARSLEY

1. Rinse the shiitakes quickly under cold water to remove any dust, then soak in 1 cup of hot water or stock for 30 minutes, or until soft. Squeeze the shiitakes to remove any soaking liquid and reserve the liquid for the soup. Remove and discard the tough stems, thinly slice the caps, and set aside.

2. In a 4-quart saucepan, heat the oil over medium-high heat. Add the celery, shallot, garlic, leek and shiitakes. Cook, stirring often, for 2 minutes.

3. Add the fresh mushrooms to the pan and cook, stirring, for another 3 minutes.

4. Add the ginger, 3 cups of water or stock, and miso, if desired. Bring to a simmer, reduce the heat to low, and continue to simmer for 15 minutes.

5. Serve in warmed soup cups or bowls and garnish with garlic stems or chives and celery leaves or parsley.

NOTE: Dried shiitakes and miso are flavor-packed pantry staples that add a subtle depth of flavor—*umami*—to any broth or sauce. They are available in Asian markets.

VARIATION

✦ Add a 4-inch piece of seaweed (konbu) to the soup instead of the miso paste.

MIXED SEAFOOD STEAMED IN PARCHMENT WITH SHALLOTS AND WHITE WINE

❋ SERVES 6 ❋

DEBORAH REMEMBERS . . . *Ah, this dish triggers a memory of embarrassment. There was a time when I didn't know that parchment was also the cooking paper one buys in a well-stocked grocery store. On my first attempt at cooking a parchment-wrapped dish, I decided to use some of the leftover heavy paper we had from printing my husband's books and the diplomas for our School of Life students. It was a disaster! This dish, however, is lovely.*

Rush these puffy packets straight from oven to table, so each guest may enjoy the aromatic rush of steam that issues forth when the hot packets are opened. With this technique, you get a dramatic presentation for very little effort. For a truly luxurious meal, you might want to use both the lobster and fish, or substitute any seafood that catches your eye. Imagine this dish with just light vegetables such as asparagus, zucchini, and greens. Hard vegetables, such as squash, could be included but should be thinly sliced.

3 CLOVES GARLIC, PEELED AND MINCED

3 LARGE SHALLOTS, PEELED AND THINLY SLICED

3 SMALL CELERY STALKS, CUT INTO ¼-INCH DICE

2 SMALL CARROTS, PEELED AND CUT INTO ½-INCH DICE

4 TABLESPOONS EXTRA-VIRGIN OLIVE OIL

½ CUP FRESH FLAT-LEAF PARSLEY LEAVES, ROUGHLY CHOPPED

2 TABLESPOONS FRESH DILL, ROUGHLY CHOPPED

2 TABLESPOONS PAPRIKA

2 TABLESPOONS LOW-SODIUM SOY SAUCE

2 TABLESPOONS WHITE WINE

6 LARGE SCALLOPS, CUT INTO 2 PIECES EACH

1½ POUNDS SALMON OR 3 LOBSTER TAILS, SHELLED, CUT INTO 6 EQUAL PIECES

12 LARGE SHRIMP, SHELLED

FRESH BASIL, PARSLEY, AND DILL LEAVES (OPTIONAL)

6 THIN SLICES LEMON OR LIME (OPTIONAL)

1. Preheat the oven to 350 degrees F.

2. In a medium bowl, combine the garlic, shallots, celery, carrots, 2 tablespoons olive oil, parsley, and dill.

3. In a large bowl, combine the paprika, soy sauce, 2 tablespoons olive oil, and wine. Add the scallops, salmon, or lobster, and shrimp and toss to coat. (The seafood may be marinated ahead of time and refrigerated for up to 8 hours.)

4. Cut parchment paper or heavy aluminum foil into six 14-inch squares. Fold the squares in half to crease, then unfold. Divide the marinated vegetables among the packets, placing them to one side of the crease. Set 2 shrimp, 2 scallops, and a piece of salmon or lobster on top of the vegetables. If desired, tuck a few herbs into the seafood and top with a slice of lemon or lime.

5. Fold the parchment loosely over the seafood, roll the edges together, and crimp to secure. Set the packages on a large baking sheet. Bake for 20 to 25 minutes.

6. Set the packages on individual plates and serve right away, while very hot. Open the packages at the table, either by unfolding or by cutting an X in the parchment with scissors.

PESTO LINGUINE WITH LEMON ZEST, SUN-DRIED TOMATO, AND SNOW PEAS

❋ SERVES 6 ❋

Spring peas are among the first vegetables to be harvested, and every bit of the plant is delightful: the pink and white flowering pea vines that cluster along the fences by La Cocina, attracting bees and butterflies; the leafy springing tendrils, the tender, edible shoots, and the crunchy fresh peas themselves. This quick pasta combines snow peas with tart sun-dried tomatoes, olives, and a last-minute dusting of fine lemon zest. The whole dish comes together in the time that it takes the pasta to cook.

TRES ESTRELLAS PESTO

1 CUP FRESH BASIL LEAVES

1 CLOVE GARLIC, PEELED, OR MORE TO TASTE

1 TABLESPOON PINE NUTS

2 TABLESPOONS EXTRA-VIRGIN OLIVE OIL

1/4 TEASPOON SALT

LINGUINE

8 OUNCES DRIED LINGUINE

1 TEASPOON EXTRA-VIRGIN OLIVE OIL

1/4 CUP FINELY DICED RED ONION, 1/4 INCH

1 1/2 CUPS SUN-DRIED TOMATOES, CUT INTO 1/2-INCH PIECES

1/4 CUP PITTED KALAMATA OLIVES, ROUGHLY CHOPPED

1 CUP DICED FRESH TOMATOES (2 ROMA TOMATOES PEELED, CORED, AND DICED)

1/2 CUP SNOW OR SUGAR SNAP PEAS, CUT LENGTHWISE INTO STRIPS

1 LARGE LEMON

1. In the bowl of a food processor, combine the basil, garlic, pine nuts, 2 tablespoons oil, and salt. Pulse to a smooth paste, scraping down the sides of the bowl frequently.

2. Bring 4 quarts of lightly salted water to a boil. Add the linguine and stir once to separate. Return to a boil and cook for 5 to 7 minutes.

3. While the linguine is cooking, heat the remaining teaspoon olive oil in a 10-inch sauté pan over medium heat.

Add the onion, sun-dried tomatoes, and olives, and cook, stirring, for 1 minute.

4. Add fresh tomatoes and peas, and cook 1 minute more, stirring gently.

5. Drain the cooked pasta and toss immediately with the basil pesto. Add the vegetables and toss to combine. Divide the linguine among 6 warmed plates and, with a fine grater or Microplane, zest the lemon right onto the hot pasta.

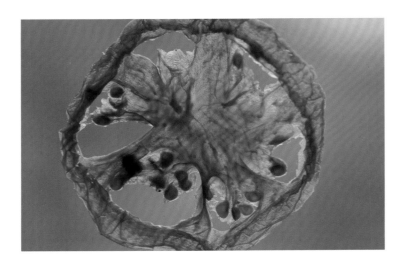

AVOCADO SORBET IN PAPAYA WITH AGED BALSAMIC VINEGAR

❋ SERVES 6 ❋

Avocados are actually a fruit. Their buttery texture and mild flavor work beautifully in sweet preparations like this sumptuous sorbet, pale green against coral pink Mexican papaya. Lime juice and a thin drizzle of good-quality aged balsamic vinegar lifts the flavors to new heights. The fat in avocado is good for you, but do serve small scoops—it's very rich. Make the avocado sorbet one or two days before you need it, to ripen the flavors.

1 MEDIUM HASS AVOCADO, PITTED

1 CUP MILK

2 1/2 OUNCES CREAM CHEESE OR MILD, CREAMY GOAT CHEESE

3 TABLESPOONS BROWN SUGAR

1 TABLESPOON GRAND MARNIER OR OTHER ORANGE LIQUEUR

1 1/2 TEASPOONS PURE VANILLA EXTRACT

1/2 TEASPOON GROUND CINNAMON

1 SMALL MEXICAN PAPAYA

1/4 CUP GOOD QUALITY IMPORTED 25-YEAR-OLD BALSAMIC VINEGAR (SEE NOTE)

1 LIME, CUT INTO 6 WEDGES

1. Cut avocados in half. Remove pit. Scoop the flesh from the avocado using a spoon and place it along with the milk, cream cheese, brown sugar, liqueur, vanilla, and cinnamon in a blender. Puree until smooth.

2. Freeze the puree in an ice cream maker according to the manufacturer's directions. If you do not have an ice cream maker, refer to the pan method in step 2 for Coconut Ice with Chocolate Drizzle and Peanuts (page 125).

3. Peel the papaya, cut it in half, and scoop out the black seeds. (The seeds are peppery and crunchy, and may be used to garnish the sorbet.) Cut the papaya into neat, small cubes.

4. Pour a teaspoon of balsamic vinegar into the bottom of a martini glass or small bowl. Top with some papaya and a scoop of sorbet, and garnish with a lime wedge. Serve immediately.

NOTE: Italian aged balsamic vinegar is tart, fruity, and complex—the perfect counterpoint to the natural richness of the avocado. Small bottles may be purchased at gourmet food shops. It is expensive, but worth the indulgence.

VARIATIONS

✦ Drizzle the balsamic directly over the sorbet.

✦ Substitute seasonal fruit such as sliced strawberries for the papaya.

"TRAVELERS, THERE IS NO PATH.
PATHS ARE MADE BY WALKING."
ANTONIO MACHADO

Head gardener Salvador Tinajero is king of summer: Everything he works for every day of the year in Tres Estrellas explodes into lush, green-leafed perfection at the height of this season. ✦ Winter rains return in summer in the form of light, juicy foods—melon and watermelon, stone fruit and tomatoes, soft vegetables and herbs—that are exactly what you want to eat in the summer heat. Everything is so fresh and tender that cooking can almost be an afterthought. ✦ In the coolness of early dawn, gardeners harvest baby vegetables, peaches, plums, grapes, and heat-loving berries and greens. This is the time to pick herbs—frilled and dappled basils, oregano, delicious mint, lemon balm, and lavender—when they are full of dewy oils. ✦ In the warming hours of midmorning, a pergola draped with pink honeysuckle smells so beautiful that it stops you in your tracks. Afternoons are never un-

SUMMER
The Dance

bearably hot because of the ocean breezes and altitude, but shade is desirable after lunch. The clean, piercing smell of Jerusalem sage fills the air, its fog-colored, flannel-soft leaves and yellow flowers crawling with bees. Heat-loving herbs like rosemary droop and sprawl, tipped with tiny blue blossoms. Tall elegant lavender with its purple spears and piercing aroma glows in the sun. After sunset, in the coolness of night, the scent of jasmine is everywhere. ✦ Early morning is the time to think about cooking. Long, drowsy afternoons are better for lolling in a hammock under the trees with a big jug of chilled *agua fresca* (see page 34) nearby. But when the sun goes down, it's time to fire up the grill and toss a salad. Summertime is for easy living—lazy days with friends and family, spur-of-the-moment get-togethers, and languid, romantic evenings under the summer stars.

LOBSTER PAELLA PARTY

·✦·

MEDITERRANEAN SALAD

GOLDEN MELON GAZPACHO SHOTS

LOBSTER AND SHRIMP PAELLA

TRIO OF BLACKBERRY, PLUM, AND PEACH SORBETS

·✦·

Summer in the Guadalupe Valley winemaking region brings las fiestas de las vendimias, a monthlong fiesta celebrated at wineries throughout the valley whose last event is a spectacular all-day paella competition. Huge seafood paellas heaped with local Pacific lobsters, shrimp, fish, and shellfish are cooked over roaring grapevine fires and samples are served to the hundreds in attendance along with tastings of local wines. This much smaller version of paella is surprisingly easy to make and impressively delicious. Here, too, is all the generosity of the summer garden in a bountiful tomato and cucumber salad, ripe melon gazpacho shots, and blushing stone-fruit sorbets—a menu of ultimate coolness.

MEDITERRANEAN SALAD

Tomatoes, the most seasonal of treats, are the pride of Tres Estrellas' gardeners, who grow dozens of different varieties throughout the long growing season. Ripe and juicy from the summer sun, bushels of tomatoes of all shapes, sizes, and colors arrive every morning in the Ranch kitchen. They are never, ever refrigerated, but are instead immediately turned into delicious salads like this one—a classic mixture of tomatoes, cucumbers, and feta cheese that improves after it is made.

4 LARGE, RIPE TOMATOES, CORED AND CUT INTO 1-INCH CUBES

1/4 MEDIUM RED ONION, THINLY SLICED

1 MEDIUM CUCUMBER, PEELED, SEEDED, AND CUT INTO 1-INCH CUBES

1 YELLOW OR GREEN BELL PEPPER, SEEDED AND CUT INTO 1/2-INCH PIECES

2 TABLESPOONS EXTRA-VIRGIN OLIVE OIL

2 TABLESPOONS BALSAMIC VINEGAR, OR TO TASTE

1/2 TEASPOON SEA SALT

1/4 TEASPOON FRESH GROUND BLACK PEPPER

1/2 CUP FETA OR COTIJA CHEESE, CRUMBLED

1. In a medium bowl, combine the tomatoes, onion, cucumber, and bell pepper. Add the oil, vinegar, salt, and black pepper, and stir gently. Let stand at room temperature for 30 minutes before serving.

2. Divide the salad among 6 chilled plates and sprinkle each serving with 2 tablespoons feta.

VARIATIONS

✦ For an even simpler salad, choose a variety of colors and flavors of tomatoes. Slice tomatoes thinly and layer on a platter. Drizzle with olive oil and balsamic vinegar, sprinkle with salt and pepper, and crumble the feta cheese over the entire salad.

✦ Add good Greek or Spanish olives, either black or green.

GOLDEN MELON GAZPACHO SHOTS

❋ SERVES 6 ❋

A ripe summer melon is a glorious thing. Make this cooling gazpacho with the best ripe melon you can find; orange-fleshed cantaloupe, muskmelons, sweet honeydews, and casaba melons are all good choices. (Jesús sometimes adds other ripe fruit, such as peaches, mangoes, and figs to the gazpacho.) A ripe melon should be heavy, and a bit soft at the stem end. It should smell wonderful, even before you cut into it—the ultimate test for ripeness.

1 RIPE CANTALOUPE OR SIMILAR MUSKMELON, PEELED AND SEEDED (ABOUT 4 1/2 CUPS)

1/2 CUP LIGHT COCONUT MILK, FRESH COCONUT JUICE, OR WATER

1/4 CUP FRESH LIME JUICE, OR TO TASTE

1/2 TEASPOON GROUND CALIFORNIA CHILE

1/4 TEASPOON GROUND CINNAMON

1/2 TEASPOON SALT

1/2 CUP PEELED, SEEDED, AND DICED CUCUMBER

2 TABLESPOONS CHOPPED FRESH MINT, LEMON BALM, OR LEMON VERBENA LEAVES

1 TEASPOON AGAVE SYRUP, OR TO TASTE

LIME WEDGES

1. Set aside about 1/2 cup of the melon. Roughly chop the rest. You should have about 4 cups. In a blender, puree thoroughly with the coconut milk, lime juice, ground chile, cinnamon, and salt.

2. Cut the reserved melon into 1/4-inch dice, and add it to a medium bowl along with the cucumber, 1 tablespoon of the herbs, and the agave syrup. Taste the gazpacho at this point—you may want to add a little more lime juice or agave. Remember that chilling will dull the flavor slightly.

3. Chill the gazpacho for at least 3 hours. Meanwhile, place 6 straight-sided tequila glasses or small shot glasses in the freezer to chill. To serve, stir the gazpacho well. Ladle into chilled glasses. Sprinkle with the remaining 1 tablespoon of herbs, and garnish with a wedge of lime perched on each glass.

LOBSTER AND SHRIMP PAELLA

❧ SERVES 6 ❧

DEBORAH REMEMBERS . . . *Seafood paella is the perfect dish for entertaining. I did a lot of paellas in the early days at my house on Dove Street in San Diego. It's part of my repertoire, so to speak, and some friends tell me I'm quite renowned for it. Add the fish and the green peas at the very end—it's really quite an artful piece.*

Great paella is carefully built on successive layers of flavors, starting with a *sofrito* of aromatic ingredients, then adding and toasting the rice, stirring in a golden saffron stock, and finally crowning the whole with an assortment of fresh shellfish and vegetables.

Traditional paella is cooked on a low grill over a hot wood fire. In this foolproof method, you will start on top of the stove and finish in the oven. Build the paella in any wide, shallow ovenproof sauté pan—even a large frying pan will do, so long as it is at least 12 inches wide and no more than 3 inches deep. The recipe may also be halved and cooked in a 10-inch pan. Always allow the paella to rest after cooking, no matter how eager you are to dive in.

1 TEASPOON SPANISH SAFFRON THREADS

1/4 CUP HOT WATER

1 TABLESPOON OLIVE OIL

2 POBLANO CHILES, SEEDED AND CUT INTO 1/4-INCH DICE

10 CLOVES GARLIC, PEELED AND MINCED

1/2 WHITE ONION, PEELED AND CUT INTO 1/4-INCH DICE

1 LEEK, WHITE PART ONLY, WASHED AND CUT INTO 1/2-INCH PIECES

4 OUNCES SMALL BAY SHRIMP, DRAINED

4 OUNCES SMALL BAY SCALLOPS, DRAINED

2 CUPS LONG-GRAIN BROWN RICE

3 ROMA TOMATOES, SEEDED AND CUT INTO 1/4-INCH DICE

1 CUP WHITE WINE

3 CUPS BASIC VEGETABLE STOCK (PAGE 176) OR WATER

1/2 TEASPOON SEA SALT

1 LARGE LOBSTER, SPLIT, OR 6 SMALL SLIPPER LOBSTER TAILS, SHELLS SPLIT

6 LARGE SHRIMP, PEELED AND DEVEINED

6 LARGE CLAMS OR 6 BLACK MUSSELS, WELL SCRUBBED

1 RED BELL PEPPER, ROASTED (SEE PAGE 108), PEELED, AND CUT INTO JULIENNE

1/2 TEASPOON SPANISH PAPRIKA

1/2 CUP COOKED GREEN PEAS

LEMON WEDGES

1. Preheat the oven to 375 degrees F.

2. Soak the saffron in the hot water for 30 minutes.

3. In a 12-inch ovenproof sauté pan, heat the olive oil over medium heat. Sauté the chiles, stirring often, until soft, about 2 minutes. Add the garlic, onion, and leek, and cook, stirring for 2 minutes more.

4. Add the shrimp and scallops and cook, stirring, for 1 minute.

5. Stir in the rice, then the tomatoes, and cook for 1 minute more.

6. Reduce the heat to low and add the saffron liquid. Rinse the saffron container with the wine, and add that

to the pan. Add the stock and salt, and stir gently but thoroughly to combine.

7. Bring the paella almost to a boil; shake the pan gently, but do not stir.

8. Move the paella to the oven and bake, uncovered, for 20 minutes. Remove from the oven and set the lobster, shrimp, clams or mussels, and pepper on top. Sprinkle the seafood with paprika and return to the oven for 15 to 20 minutes more, or until the seafood is just cooked. (Be careful not to overcook.)

9. Remove from the oven and set on the range top, where the paella will stay warm. Scatter the peas over the paella. Drape the paella with a clean kitchen towel and let it rest for 15 minutes to soften the rice and seafood.

10. Serve with lemon wedges.

NOTE: Because this paella uses brown rice, outdoor cooking is not recommended, as the rice will not cook evenly.

VARIATIONS

✦ To make a quick paella, make the rice with the *sofrito* in a pot or on the stove top. Stir in already sautéed vegetables and arrange sautéed or baked seafood on top. This is cheating, but it works.

✦ Substitute assorted grilled vegetables, cut into pieces, for the seafood and add during the last 5 minutes of cooking.

✦ Use both slipper lobster tails and the whole lobster.

✦ Substitute 6 small pieces of fish for the lobster or shrimp.

✦ Make a Baja-style paella with whole small blue crabs, baby calamari, and octopus.

✦ Jesús sometimes makes paella with half the rice and twice the vegetables.

TRIO OF BLACKBERRY, PLUM, AND PEACH SORBETS

❧ SERVES 6 ❧

Blushing peach, deep purple, and pale pink, a trio of pretty sorbets is a special finish to a summer meal. At the Ranch, these fruit sorbets are made from the very ripest plums, blackberries, and peaches, brought to the kitchen still warm from the sun and absolutely bursting with flavor. Any summer fruit at its flavorful best will make a wonderful sorbet: strawberries, melons of all kinds, raspberries, apricots. Even tart cherries are well worth the work to prepare.

Choose with your nose as well as your eyes. Ripe fruit gives off a luscious perfume. You might even decide to infuse one of the sorbets with an herb from the garden—tarragon, lemon basil, mint, or rose geranium flowers are all wonderful with fruit. Garnish with a flower or herb, diced fruit, or a thin stalk of lemongrass to nibble.

2 CUPS PITTED AND CHOPPED RIPE PLUMS

2 CUPS PEELED, PITTED, AND CHOPPED RIPE PEACHES OR NECTARINES

2 CUPS RIPE BLACKBERRIES, RINSED, DRIED, AND PICKED OVER

1/2 CUP AGAVE SYRUP, MAPLE SYRUP, OR PACKED BROWN SUGAR

EDIBLE FLOWERS, HERB SPRIGS, FRESH BERRIES, MORSELS OF FRUIT, OR LEMONGRASS STALKS (OPTIONAL)

1. Wash the plums. Cut in half and remove the pits, then cut the fruit into small pieces.

2. Skin the peaches by pouring boiling water over them for 10 seconds. Cool, then remove the skin with a sharp knife. Cut in half and remove the stones, then cut the fruit into small pieces.

3. Quickly rinse, dry, and pick over the blackberries.

4. Place each fruit in a separate plastic bag and freeze overnight.

5. In the bowl of a food processor, puree each fruit separately until perfectly smooth, adding a couple of tablespoons of syrup or more if the fruit is tart, rinsing the bowl in between.

6. As you finish each puree, pack it into a small container, cover, and freeze for at least 1 hour. If the sorbet becomes very hard, let the container stand at room temperature to soften for 10 minutes.

7. Serve a small scoop of each sorbet in a chilled dessert bowl or martini glass with one or more of the garnishes, if desired.

EDIBLE FLOWERS

Jesús frequently uses flowers for color and flavor on salads and desserts. In spring, he stuffs golden zucchini flowers (*flor de calabasa*) with minced vegetables or cheeses, tucks peppery nasturtium blossoms into salads, or scatters lavender flowers over berries. He says, jokingly, that he is not allowed to touch the sweet-smelling antique floribunda roses that grown in abundance around La Cocina; they are owner Sarah Livia Brightwood's "pets." In late spring and throughout summer and fall, flowering herb tops are harvested daily for garnishes. Though often categorized as savory, most herbs taste delicious paired with berries and other fruit.

Most flowers are edible, but make sure they have been grown organically, away from animals, and free from pesticides. Swish gently in cold water just before use and drain on towels. Tiny flowers and flower bells may be used whole. The petals of larger flowers, such as calendula, add a spark of bright color to the plate. In other seasons, look for fall flowers, such as mums, which come in brilliant colors.

BORAGE	Mild cucumber flavor; use tiny blue bell clusters
CALENDULA	Use petals
CHIVE FLOWER	Pronounced onion flavor; don't use on sweets
DAISY	Use petals
GARLIC OR SOCIETY GARLIC FLOWER	Excellent soup garnish
GUAVA FLOWER	Pink and sweet tasting
LAVENDER	Fragrant and wonderful with sweet or savory dishes
MARIGOLD	Bright yellow and tangy
MUM	Brilliant colors; use petals only
NASTURTIUM	Bright color and distinct, peppery flavor
PANSY	Use small blooms
ROSE GERANIUM	Spicy, pronounced flavor; infuse and strain before use
ROSEMARY	Tender purple blossoms and tips; delicious with apples and pears
ROSE, GRANDIFLORA, AND FLORIBUNDA	Use petals for a beautiful presentation
SAGE FLOWER	Has a drop of nectar at the base
SQUASH FLOWER	Cook or chop and add to salads
VIOLET	Use small blooms; fragrant and sweet tasting

The Hottest Day of the Year

+

CUCUMBER, DILL, AND YOGURT SALAD WITH RED PEPPER

GRILLED SHRIMP ON LOCAL MELON WITH TAMARIND SAUCE

GRILLED BABY VEGETABLES

BLACK QUINOA TABBOULEH

GRILLED FIGS WITH CREAMY HONEYED RICOTTA AND ALMONDS

+

On the hottest of summer days, when you can barely lift a hand to fan yourself and the dog lies panting in the dirt, what you need is something light, refreshing, and easy. When the sun goes down and cool breezes finally spring up, a few minutes of grill time are all that's required to get this dinner on the table.

CUCUMBER, DILL, AND YOGURT SALAD WITH RED PEPPER

❋ SERVES 6 ❋

Cucumbers and dill, a classic combination, are given a La Cocina twist here with crisp fennel and roasted red peppers in a tangy yogurt dressing. The salad is even better when made several hours or a day ahead. Jesús sometimes adds juicy fresh fennel seeds, ground fennel seeds, or a sprinkling of fennel pollen (available in gourmet specialty stores) to enhance the flavor of the fresh fennel.

1 LARGE OR 2 SMALL CUCUMBERS, PEELED

2 TEASPOONS SEA SALT

1 RED BELL PEPPER, ROASTED (SEE PAGE 108), PEELED, AND CUT INTO THIN STRIPS

1/2 SMALL FENNEL BULB, THINLY SLICED

1/4 SMALL RED ONION, THINLY SLICED

1/4 CUP FRESH DILL, CHOPPED

1 1/2 CUPS PLAIN BALKAN-STYLE (THICK) YOGURT

1/4 TEASPOON FRESH GROUND BLACK PEPPER, OR TO TASTE

1. Cut each cucumber in half lengthwise. Remove seeds if necessary, then cut into thin slices. In a large bowl, toss the cucumber with 1 teaspoon of salt and set aside for 30 minutes. (The salt will draw some of the moisture from the cucumber and soften the slices.) Rinse and drain thoroughly.

2. Add the bell pepper, fennel, red onion, dill, and yogurt, and mix well. Season with the remaining teaspoon of salt and the pepper to taste. Refrigerate the salad for several hours. Stir well before serving.

VARIATIONS

✦ Leave the red pepper raw, and cut into dice or julienne.

✦ Substitute thinly sliced celery for the fennel.

✦ For a more substantial salad, serve on a bed of baby greens and sprinkle with toasted pine nuts.

✦ Jesús sometimes adds 1 teaspoon wasabi powder mixed with 1 teaspoon water to form a paste to the salad.

YOGURT

If you like yogurt, take a good look at the ingredients on a package of typical supermarket yogurt. There's very little that's good for you in that long list: high-fructose corn syrup, flavorings, gums, and preservatives. Choose wisely! Healthy yogurt is simple and fresh tasting, packed with live cultures. The best quality yogurts are thick and tangy Mediterranean-style yogurts, which may be labeled Greek, Russian, or Balkan. You can make fresh yogurt at home in an inexpensive (and foolproof) yogurt maker, which keeps the yogurt at exactly the right temperature while it thickens. Yogurt may be sweetened—if at all—with fresh fruit puree, agave syrup, or a touch of honey. Drained yogurt, or *labna,* is thick and creamy-smooth, a perfect substitute for sour cream or crème fraîche.

GRILLED SHRIMP ON LOCAL MELON
WITH TAMARIND SAUCE

※ SERVES 6 ※

Summer cooking doesn't get much easier—or prettier—than this combination of warm grilled shrimp in a tart-sweet marinade on cool greens with a delicious, juicy melon from the farmers' market. A touch of fresh lime juice brings out the subtle flavor of the fruit; green pepitas add crunch.

18 LARGE SHRIMP, PREFERABLY WILD

1 1/2 CUPS TAMARIND SAUCE (RECIPE FOLLOWS)

1 LARGE RIPE LOCAL MELON, PREFERABLY WITH ORANGE FLESH, PEELED, SEEDED, AND CUT INTO 1-INCH CUBES

4 TABLESPOONS FRESH LIME JUICE

3 CUPS PEPPERY GREENS, SUCH AS BABY ARUGULA, SPINACH, OR WATERCRESS, STEMMED

2 TABLESPOONS EXTRA-VIRGIN OLIVE OIL

2 TABLESPOONS FRESH ORANGE JUICE

1/4 CUP TOASTED GREEN PEPITAS (PUMPKIN SEEDS) OR PINE NUTS

2 GREEN ONIONS, FINELY SLICED

1. Peel the shrimp. (You may leave the tails on or remove them.) Toss the shrimp with about ½ cup sauce, enough to coat the shrimp. Slip 3 shrimp onto each of 6 wooden or metal skewers. Wrap and refrigerate until ready to grill.

2. Toss the melon with 2 tablespoons of the lime juice and refrigerate.

3. Place the greens in a bowl, cover, and chill until ready to use.

4. About 15 minutes before serving, preheat a gas grill or grill pan. Grill the shrimp for 3 minutes per side, or until cooked through and just firm. Do not overcook.

5. While the shrimp are cooking, toss the greens with the olive oil, remaining 2 tablespoons of lime juice, and the orange juice. Divide the greens among 6 plates and spoon some melon on top of the greens.

6. Thin the remaining cup of sauce with a small amount of water until it is thin enough to drizzle.

7. Set the cooked shrimp on top of the melon and drizzle each serving with about 2 tablespoons of the sauce. Scatter a few bright green pepitas and green onions on the salad.

VARIATIONS

✦ Instead of shrimp, substitute any kind of fish, grilled vegetables (especially eggplant, peppers, and zucchini), or grilled firm tofu.

✦ Substitute coral-colored Mexican papaya or ripe mango for the melon.

✦ Skewer with 1-inch cubes of summer squash, bell peppers, onion, or cherry tomatoes.

✦ Instead of grilling, bake the shrimp in a 350-degree F oven until pink and firm.

TAMARIND SAUCE

✳ MAKES 3 CUPS ✳

Tamarind Sauce has a sweet-tart flavor that finds many uses as a sauce on stir-fried vegetables or noodles, as a dip for raw vegetables, or on anything grilled, especially fish. Thin the sauce with water and use as a salad dressing. Any extra will keep, refrigerated, for up to 2 weeks, or frozen for up to 2 months. Tamarind paste is sold in Asian markets.

14 OUNCES SEEDLESS TAMARIND PASTE

3 CUPS WATER

1/2 CUP LOW-SODIUM SOY SAUCE

1/2 CUP MIRIN RICE WINE

1/2 CUP RICE VINEGAR

1 CINNAMON STICK

1 STAR ANISE

3/4 CUP PACKED BROWN SUGAR

1/4 CUP FRESH CILANTRO LEAVES, CHOPPED

1/4 CUP SLICED GREEN ONION TOPS

2 CLOVES GARLIC, PEELED AND MINCED

1. Break the tamarind paste into small pieces and place in a 2-quart saucepan. Add the water and bring to a boil over medium heat. Remove from the heat and let soak for 30 minutes, then mash the tamarind with a stiff whisk or potato masher until it forms a paste, adding a little more water as needed.

2. Add the soy sauce, rice wine, rice vinegar, cinnamon stick, anise, and brown sugar, and cook over medium-low heat for 30 minutes, stirring occasionally.

3. Turn off heat. Remove the cinnamon stick and star anise. Use the back of a serving spoon or a rubber spatula to rub the paste through a coarse sieve. Stir in the cilantro, green onions, and garlic, and thin as neccessary with water.

GRILLING INDOORS AND OUT

When grilling outdoors, you may cook over propane gas, seasoned wood, or wood charcoal (avoid briquettes, which are concocted of wood byproduct and powdered charcoal). Heat your grill and thoroughly clean the grill bars with a wire brush. Rub the cleaned grill with a lightly oiled paper towel. Foods to be grilled may be marinated or given a quick dry rub of spices. Lightly oil the food itself just before setting on your hot, clean, oiled grill. A grill basket is helpful when handing small items or fish.

You can also successfully grill indoors any time of year using a cast-iron grill pan on the stovetop (many have a flat side and grill side), a countertop electric grill, which cooks top and bottom at once, or a small fireplace grill that sits in your hearth. The advantage is that there is no need to light the grill to cook a small amount of food, but indoor grilling does require good ventilation.

GRILLED BABY VEGETABLES

❄ SERVES 6 ❄

Baby vegetables are a cook's delight but a gardener's headache. The problem, says Salvador, is that they are small one day but not the next, and chefs want them all the same size. Picky chefs aside, summer is the time to look for true baby vegetables at farmers' markets or in your garden.

Baby vegetables are a taste revelation when grilled. The trick is to cook them quickly over a hot fire so they retain their crunch but pick up a little smoky flavor. Little zucchini become creamy and tender. Little leeks, about the thickness of your thumb, have a sweet flavor and distinctive snap all their own. Tiny baby carrots and new onions are so sweet that it will be a wonder if any make it out of the kitchen.

Jesús likes to grill vegetables in all seasons. Particular favorites are baby potatoes, mini bell peppers, baby corn, Brussels sprouts, sliced sweet potatoes, asparagus, and eggplant, which he serves with pesto or Aztec Guacamole (page 90).

ASSORTED BABY VEGETABLES, TRIMMED AND PEELED, IF NECESSARY (ABOUT 8 TO 10 PIECES PER PERSON)

EXTRA-VIRGIN OLIVE OIL

MEDIUM-COARSE SEA SALT OR KOSHER SALT

CHOPPED FRESH HERBS, SUCH AS PARSLEY, CHIVES, CHERVIL, OR THYME

1. Build a hot fire in a grill or heat a cast-iron grill pan over high heat.

2. Toss the vegetables with enough olive oil to coat lightly, add a sprinkle of salt, and drain off any excess. Place the vegetables in a grilling basket for the outdoor grill and cook quickly on both sides. If cooking in a stovetop grill pan, set the vegetables in the pan and don't move them until they have grill marks on one side. Then shake the pan several times, cook for 1 minute more if necessary, and turn out onto a plate.

3. Sprinkle with the chopped herbs, and serve at room temperature.

NOTE: If you use an outdoor grill, a grilling basket is essential. These may be purchased at any cookware or garden store. If you don't have a grill, baby vegetables of all kinds take well to indoor grilling (page 184), pan-roasting (page 185) or searing (page 185).

BLACK QUINOA TABBOULEH

❋ SERVES 6 ❋

Lemony tabbouleh salad is a staple in Eastern Mediterranean cuisines, where it is usually made with cracked bulgur wheat. Jesús' version of tabbouleh is a nutritional powerhouse of high-protein black quinoa, lots of chopped vegetables, iron-rich parsley, and tomatoes, which makes for a dramatic presentation. Do try to find black quinoa, as it makes a beautiful salad.

1 CUP WATER

½ CUP BLACK QUINOA

1 BAY LEAF

¼ CUP TOASTED PINE NUTS

½ CUP DICED TART APPLE, SKIN ON, ¼ INCH

½ CUP DICED RED BELL PEPPER, ¼ INCH

¼ CUP DICED RED ONION, ¼ INCH

2 TABLESPOONS CHOPPED, FRESH FLAT-LEAF PARSLEY

¼ CUP EXTRA-VIRGIN OLIVE OIL

3 TABLESPOONS RED WINE VINEGAR

SALT AND FRESH GROUND PEPPER TO TASTE

1. In a small saucepan, combine the water, quinoa, and bay leaf, and bring to a boil over medium-high heat. Reduce the heat to medium-low, cover, and cook for 15 minutes.

2. Remove from heat, shake to loosen the grains, and cool to room temperature with the lid ajar.

3. In a medium-sized bowl, combine the pine nuts, apple, bell pepper, red onion, and parsley. Add the quinoa and stir.

4. Just before serving, whisk the olive oil and vinegar together, pour over the quinoa, and toss to combine. Season to taste.

VARIATION

✦ Substitute white quinoa, bulgur, barley, any kind of rice, or whole wheat couscous for the black quinoa. For directions on cooking these grains, see Basics on page 165.

GRILLED FIGS WITH CREAMY HONEYED RICOTTA AND ALMONDS

❋ SERVES 6 ❋

The green-skinned, pink-fleshed mission figs that grow throughout the Baja California region were one of the four historical gifts (figs, wheat, grapes, and olives) planted at every settlement by Spanish missionaries in the eighteenth century. The missions are long gone, but the figs still thrive in the arid heat, offering shade throughout the hot summers and sweet fruit to eat fresh or to dry in the sun.

Cook the figs while you are enjoying dinner, either on the grill for a smoky-sweet flavor or wrapped in foil and cooked in the last of the embers. Apricots, plums, nectarines, and peaches are also great cooked in this manner.

½ CUP RICOTTA CHEESE

½ CUP CREAM CHEESE (SEE NOTE)

4 TABLESPOONS HONEY, PLUS MORE TO TASTE

2 TABLESPOONS FRESH LEMON JUICE

1 TEASPOON PURE VANILLA EXTRACT OR ANISE- OR FRUIT-FLAVORED LIQUEUR, OR A COMBINATION OF THE TWO (OPTIONAL)

18 RIPE FIGS

1 TEASPOON OLIVE OIL

¼ CUP TOASTED ALMONDS

1. In a blender or food processor, puree the ricotta, cream cheese, honey, lemon juice, and vanilla, if desired, until perfectly smooth. Taste and add more honey or vanilla to taste—the cream should have lots of flavor. For the finest texture, press the cream through a fine-mesh sieve.

2. Clean the figs with a dampened paper towel, pat dry, and rub with the olive oil. Skewer and grill over medium heat for 3 minutes, or until heated through and lightly roasted. If you prefer, the figs may be wrapped in foil packets and cooked, turning several times, over the flames or tucked in the coals. This will take about 5 minutes.

3. Split almost in half and top with 1 tablespoon of the Honeyed Ricotta. Serve warm with a few almonds scattered on each plate.

NOTE: For a thicker, creamier texture, add up to ¼ cup more cream cheese.

SUMMER NIGHTS

GRILLED WHITE CORN SOUP
WITH LEEKS AND ROASTED PEPPERS

POACHED WILD SALMON
WITH AVOCADO-TARRAGON AIOLI ON GREENS

NEW-POTATO SALAD WITH CHERVIL AND SHALLOTS

SUMMERY NECTARINE AND BERRY TARTLETS

This is a menu for the height of summer, when a drive in the country calls for stops at each and every farm stand along the way. Everything on this menu tastes better with time, so cook in the cool of the morning and serve as the sun sets.

GRILLED WHITE CORN SOUP
WITH LEEKS AND ROASTED PEPPERS

❋ SERVES 6 ❋

DEBORAH REMEMBERS . . . *Since we're walking down memory lane together, those of you who read this and were among those who went to the Ranch in the 1980s will remember the pathways we planted with alternating rows of tall sunflowers and corn. Well, we used that corn! It was white corn, and when we cut it off the cob, we probably ate half of it before it went into the soups. Luscious!*

In Mexico, fresh corn is roasted or grilled until smoky-sweet and deliciously chewy. For this classic chowder, the corn is pan-roasted, then cooked to a golden velvet with leeks and aromatic vegetables.

Founder Deborah and Chef Jesús like to give food a quick last touch as it is served. It might be as simple as a quick sauté of leeks, corn, and peppers for this corn soup, a drizzle of extra-virgin olive oil over tomatoes and basil, or a dash of fennel powder on grilled fish. That last touch always lifts each dish a notch, adding freshness and flavor, a hint of textural or temperature contrast, and eye appeal.

4 EARS SWEET CORN, WHITE OR YELLOW, SHUCKED AND SILK REMOVED

2 LEEKS, WHITE PART ONLY, WASHED AND CUT INTO ½-INCH DICE

1 RED BELL PEPPER, ROASTED (SEE PAGE 108), PEELED, SEEDED, AND CUT INTO ½-INCH DICE

2½ TEASPOONS OLIVE OIL, PLUS MORE FOR THE PAN

½ STALK CELERY, MINCED

1 CLOVE GARLIC, PEELED AND MINCED

5 CUPS BASIC VEGETABLE STOCK (PAGE 176) OR WATER

1 TEASPOON FRESH THYME LEAVES

1 BAY LEAF

1 TEASPOON SALT, OR MORE TO TASTE

¼ TEASPOON FRESH GROUND BLACK PEPPER

1 TABLESPOON MINCED CHIVES

1. Over a medium bowl, cut off the corn kernels with a sharp knife. You should have about 2½ cups.

2. In a lightly oiled heavy-bottomed sauté pan, sear the corn in batches over medium heat until it has a few black spots.

3. Set aside ½ cup of the corn and ¼ cup each of the diced leeks and peppers. In a 4-quart pot, heat 2 teaspoons of the olive oil over medium heat. Add the remaining corn, leeks, peppers, celery, and garlic. Cook slowly, stirring often, for 5 minutes. Add the stock, thyme, bay leaf, and salt.

4. Cook until the vegetables are tender. Remove the bay leaf. In a blender or food processor, puree soup until smooth. Add the black pepper and taste for seasoning, adding more salt, if desired.

5. Just before serving, sauté the reserved corn, leeks, and peppers in the remaining ½ teaspoon of olive oil, and add them to the hot soup. To serve, ladle the soup into 6 warmed bowls and garnish with a pinch of chives.

VARIATION

✦ Jesús likes to puree the soup until absolutely smooth and serve it cold, garnished with reserved roasted red pepper and chives.

POACHED WILD SALMON
WITH AVOCADO-TARRAGON AIOLI
ON GREENS

❋ SERVES 6 ❋

In the age of the grill, the subtle and simple art of poaching is worth rediscovering. Slow-cooking in a wine-laced, aromatic herb court bouillon keeps fish moist and delicious. Choose a wild troll-caught salmon or substitute other firm seafood, such as fresh Alaskan halibut or shrimp.

French tarragon is finicky, delicate, and difficult to grow (Tres Estrellas has one tiny, precious plot), but it's worth the effort. It has a distinctive, almost lemony flavor that holds its own with the rich salmon and avocado.

2 BAY LEAVES

3 SPRIGS FRESH DILL

2 SPRIGS FRESH BASIL, TOPS ONLY

2 SPRIGS FRESH FLAT-LEAF PARSLEY

2 THIN SLICES WHITE ONION

2 SLICES LEMON, LIME, OR LEMONGRASS

5 WHOLE BLACK PEPPERCORNS

1/4 TEASPOON SEA SALT

1/2 CUP WHITE WINE OR APPLE CIDER

1/2 CUP WATER

6 PIECES FRESH WILD SALMON, ABOUT 5 OUNCES EACH

BASIL-BALSAMIC DRESSING (PAGE 79)

6 CUPS MIXED GREENS

AVOCADO-TARRAGON AIOLI (RECIPE FOLLOWS)

6 FRESH TARRAGON SPRIGS OR FENNEL TOPS (OPTIONAL)

6 LEMON WEDGES

1. In a large sauté pan, combine the herbs, onion, lemon, peppercorns, salt, wine, and water, and bring almost to a boil over medium-high heat, to make a court bouillon. Reduce the heat to low and simmer for about 3 minutes.

2. Add the salmon and continue to cook the fish with the lid ajar over low heat for 10 to 12 minutes, or until the fish flakes easily with a fork or reaches an internal temperature of 140 degrees F. Be careful not to overcook the fish (see Note) or allow the court bouillon to boil. Cool the salmon in the court bouillon.

3. When cool, remove from pan carefully with a slotted spatula or spoon. (The fish may be made ahead to this point and refrigerated, wrapped, for up to 24 hours.)

4. Lightly dress the greens and divide among 6 plates. Set a piece of salmon on the greens. Spoon about 1½ tablespoons of the aioli on the salmon, or serve on the side. Add a sprig of tarragon for color, if desired, and serve with a lemon wedge.

NOTE: As a rule of thumb, fish needs to be cooked for 10 minutes per inch (measured at the thickest part). Fully cooked fish will flake when gently pressed with a finger. Undercooked fish will still feel soft in the middle. All fish are moister when slightly undercooked.

VARIATION

✦ Serve atop thinly sliced ripe tomatoes, drizzled with a touch of aged balsamic vinegar.

AVOCADO-TARRAGON AIOLI

❊ MAKES ³/₄ CUP ❊

Sauces should be assertively flavored and served in small portions. This avocado-based aioli has plenty of punch to set off the mild flavor of the salmon, and the colors—pale green on pink—are really beautiful together. This aioli is also wonderful with raw or cooked vegetables or simple grilled shrimp.

1 SOFT-RIPE HASS AVOCADO, PITTED AND PEELED

1 CLOVE GARLIC, PEELED

1 SMALL SHALLOT, PEELED

¹/₂ TEASPOON TARRAGON VINEGAR OR WHITE WINE VINEGAR

1 TABLESPOON FRESH LEMON JUICE

¹/₂ TEASPOON SEA SALT (OPTIONAL)

1 TABLESPOON CHOPPED FRESH CHIVES

2 SPRIGS FRESH FLAT-LEAF PARSLEY, STEMMED AND CHOPPED (ABOUT 2 TEASPOONS)

1 SPRIG FRESH TARRAGON, STEMMED AND CHOPPED (ABOUT 1 TEASPOON)

1. At least 3 hours before serving, puree the avocado with the garlic and shallot in the bowl of a food processor until perfectly smooth.

2. Scrape the puree into a small bowl and stir in the vinegar, lemon juice, and salt, if desired. Taste for seasoning; it should taste quite strong.

3. Stir in the chopped herbs, cover, and refrigerate until serving time.

NEW-POTATO SALAD
WITH CHERVIL AND SHALLOTS

❋ SERVES 6 ❋

According to Jesús, little purple shallots—sweet little onions with a gentle taste of garlic—are a gift from *"la tierra natural."* Shallots grow in abundance at Tres Estrellas and are always his preference when cooking or making salad dressings. It's well worth finding fresh shallots, or you may substitute a sweet red onion, such as a torpedo onion, or Maui, Vidalia, or Texas sweet onions.

Jesús is also crazy about chervil, a finicky and fragile herb that gives Salvador fits when he tries to grow it in the heat. If you can't find chervil, substitute flat-leaf Italian parsley or tender celery leaves.

1½ POUNDS SMALL OR NEW POTATOES, SUCH AS RED, PURPLE, FINGERLING, OR YUKON GOLD

¼ CUP SHALLOTS, PEELED AND CUT INTO SMALL DICE

¼ CUP CHOPPED FRESH CHERVIL, FLAT-LEAF PARSLEY, OR TENDER CELERY LEAVES

VINAIGRETTE

1 TABLESPOON MINCED SHALLOTS

¼ CUP RED WINE VINEGAR

½ TEASPOON SALT

⅛ TEASPOON FRESH GROUND BLACK PEPPER

2 TEASPOONS WHOLE-GRAIN MUSTARD

2 TABLESPOONS OLIVE OIL

1. Wash the potatoes. Boil the potatoes until tender (peeling is not necessary). When the potatoes are cooled, cut them in half and combine in a large bowl with the shallots and chervil.

2. In a small bowl, combine the minced shallots, vinegar, salt, and pepper. Whisk in the mustard and then the olive oil. Pour over the potatoes, toss to coat, and serve.

QUICK HERB OILS

Professional chefs use bright-green herb oils to add droplets of intense flavor to salads and sauces. To make herb-infused oil, combine 1 cup packed fresh herbs with 2 cups of olive oil in a blender, and puree until the oil turns pale green. Set a funnel over a clean jar, line the funnel with a paper coffee filter, and pour in the oil. Infused oils should be used right away, or refrigerated and used within a week.

SUMMERY NECTARINE AND BERRY TARTLETS

❋ SERVES 6 ❋

Perfect summer fruit needs no fussing or elaborate presentation to become the center of attention. Ripe nectarines and any seasonal berries will glow like jewels on this crunchy, cookie-like crust. Serve the tarts simply brushed with a little agave syrup for shine, or dressed up with a small scoop of one of the fruit sorbets on page 56 or whipped cream.

CRUST

1 CUP ROLLED OATS OR LOW-FAT GRANOLA

1/2 CUP SLICED ALMONDS

1/8 TEASPOON FRESH GRATED NUTMEG

ZEST OF 1 ORANGE

1 EGG WHITE

1/2 CUP AGAVE SYRUP OR MAPLE SYRUP

FILLING

3 RIPE NECTARINES, PITTED AND SLICED INTO 1/4-INCH WEDGES

1/2 PINT FRESH BLUEBERRIES OR RASPBERRIES

FLOWERING HERB SPRIGS, SUCH AS LAVENDER OR MINT, OR EDIBLE FLOWERS (OPTIONAL)

1. Preheat the oven to 350 degrees F.

2. In the bowl of a food processor, pulse the oats, almonds, nutmeg, and orange zest 10 times to break up the oats and nuts. Add the egg white and 1/4 cup of the agave syrup and pulse a few more times to make the dough stick together. You will still see whole bits of oat and almond.

3. Lightly oil a baking sheet, or line with a nonstick silicone mat. Set a 3 1/2-inch round cookie cutter or tart ring onto the pan. Scoop one slightly rounded tablespoon of dough into the ring. Hold the ring with one hand and carefully tamp the dough down with the back of a dampened spoon, pressing the dough to the edges of the ring to make a clean edge, then lift off the ring. Repeat until you have 12 tartlets.

4. Bake the tartlets until crisp and golden brown, 8 to 10 minutes. Immediately run a thin spatula beneath each tartlet to loosen from the pan. Cool and store in an airtight container until ready to serve. You will only need six tartlet bases for this recipe. Reserve the rest for another use.

5. Arrange the nectarine slices in an overlapping circle on each tartlet base. Set a few berries in the middle of the circle. Just before serving, brush the fruit lightly with the remaining agave syrup. Top with an herb sprig, if desired.

VARIATIONS

✦ Drizzle the baked tartlet shells with a little melted dark chocolate before topping with fruit.

✦ Substitute any sliced summer fruit—peeled and sliced apricots, pitted cherries, plums, strawberries, or figs—for the nectarines and berries.

✦ In fall and winter, top the tartlet bases with glazed sliced bananas and a drizzle of melted chocolate; diced apples or pears, sautéed with a little brown sugar and cinnamon; bright green slices of kiwi fruit; or fresh or grilled pineapple.

THE PINK MENU

SANGRIA LA PUERTA

WATERMELON AND ROASTED BEET SALAD
WITH FENNEL AND FETA

GRILLED YELLOWTAIL TUNA
ON ASIAN EDAMAME BEAN SALAD

GUAVA CRÈME BRÛLÉE

These hot-weather recipes can be almost entirely made ahead. Start your pink menu with this unusual salad, as pretty as a dessert with chunks of vividly colored beets, hot pink watermelon, and flecks of bright green arugula and pure white feta. You'll love the combination of flavors, too: sweet, juicy, earthy, and creamy. Even beet-avoiders will become believers. Follow with pink "petals" of seared rare fish on a colorful salad, and finish with a crème brûlée made with sweet, pale-pink guava.

SANGRIA LA PUERTA

Fresh juices make all the difference here. If you can't find or make fresh grape juice, white grape juice from concentrate may be substituted.

1 ORANGE, THINLY SLICED

1 LEMON, THINLY SLICED

1 BOTTLE (750 ML) LIGHT-BODIED RED WINE, SUCH AS PINOT NOIR OR BEAUJOLAIS

1 CUP FRESH GRAPE JUICE

1 CUP UNFILTERED FRESH APPLE JUICE

1/2 CUP AGAVE SYRUP

5 WHOLE STAR ANISE

3 CINNAMON STICKS

1. Wash the orange and lemon and slice thinly from end to end. Place the orange and lemon slices in a large glass pitcher, add the remaining ingredients, and stir. Chill for at least 2 hours before serving.

2. Strain the sangria and serve in tall glasses over Herb Lemon Ice Cubes (recipe follows) if you like, and garnish with a piece of soaked fruit.

VARIATIONS

✦ Substitute fresh pink grapefruit juice for the grape juice.

✦ Substitute sparkling water for the apple juice.

✦ Add ¼ cup brandy just before serving.

✦ Add a few pieces of nectarine and green apple to each glass.

HERBED LEMON ICE CUBES

These beautiful ice cubes are made from equal parts fresh lemon juice and water, plus flower petals and herbs—mint, lemon balm, tarragon, cinnamon basil, dill, and thyme.

2 CUPS FILTERED WATER

2 CUPS FRESH LEMON JUICE, STRAINED THROUGH A FINE SIEVE

ASSORTMENT OF TINY, PERFECT HERB LEAVES, FLOWERS, AND BERRIES

Combine the water and lemon juice. Pour carefully into clean ice cube trays. Set one or two leaves or flowers in each cube, and push them under the surface of the water with a skewer. Freeze overnight.

WATERMELON AND ROASTED BEET SALAD WITH FENNEL AND FETA

❋ SERVES 6 ❋

Beets come in all colors, from hot pink to candy-stripe to golden yellow. Baby beets are wonderful in this salad, but large beets are equally delicious. Whatever size or color beets you use, roast them whole, right in their well-scrubbed skins, which concentrates their natural sweetness. Jesús removes the skins from large beets after cooking, but baby beets have such thin skins that he sometimes doesn't even peel them.

3 SMALL (OR 1 LARGE) GOLDEN BEETS, TRIMMED BUT NOT PEELED

3 SMALL (OR 1 LARGE) RED OR CANDY-STRIPE BEETS, TRIMMED BUT NOT PEELED

BASIL BALSAMIC DRESSING (RECIPE FOLLOWS)

6 WEDGES WATERMELON, 1½-INCH THICK

2 CUPS ARUGULA LEAVES, STEMMED

½ SMALL FENNEL BULB, VERY THINLY SLICED

2 TO 3 OUNCES SHARP FETA CHEESE

1. Preheat the oven to 350 degrees F.

2. Set the beets in a small roasting pan and roast until tender when poked with a sharp knife. Small beets take about 20 minutes; large beets may take as long as 1 hour.

3. Cool the beets and peel. Small beets may be cut in half. Large beets may be cut into large cubes, quartered or sliced. Toss with ¼ cup of the dressing and set aside for at least 10 minutes to marinate.

4. Cut the rind from the watermelon slices and cut the watermelon into large cubes.

5. Set a few arugula leaves on each plate. Top with watermelon and beet chunks, and scatter the fennel and crumble the feta over the top. Serve with additional dressing on the side.

VARIATIONS

✦ Dark green tatsoi or any other green with character may be substituted for the arugula.

✦ Instead of fresh fennel, sprinkle the salad with a pinch of fennel pollen (available at gourmet and specialty stores).

✦ Make the salad with beets alone and grate fresh horseradish over the salad just before serving.

BASIL BALSAMIC DRESSING

❋ MAKES 1 ½ CUPS ❋

This is one of the Ranch's best dressings, full of fresh herbs from Tres Estrellas. It is wonderful on salads, of course, but equally delicious as a sauce for grilled or roasted vegetables, cooked seafood or shrimp.

1 CUP FRESH TANGERINE OR ORANGE JUICE

3 TABLESPOONS BALSAMIC VINEGAR

1 SMALL SHALLOT, PEELED AND MINCED (ABOUT 1 TABLESPOON)

1 CLOVE GARLIC, PEELED AND MINCED (ABOUT 1 TEASPOON)

1 TABLESPOON OLIVE OIL

¼ TEASPOON FRESH GROUND BLACK PEPPER

¼ TEASPOON SEA SALT, OR MORE TO TASTE

4 LARGE LEAVES FRESH BASIL, CHOPPED (ABOUT 1 TABLESPOON)

6 SPRIGS FRESH CILANTRO, STEMMED AND CHOPPED (ABOUT 1 TABLESPOON)

1 TEASPOON CHOPPED FRESH THYME LEAVES

One hour before serving, whisk together all ingredients. Taste and add salt, if needed.

SEASONALITY

Deborah Szekely says seasonality is nature giving you what you need when you need it. This is a simple rule for eating naturally and healthfully— locally grown foods, in season, always taste the best and are the best for you. Truly seasonal foods, such as tomatoes, may be available year-round, but they never taste as good as they do during their natural season. Research what's grown in your area and when it is in season, and build your menus around those things.

The best way to find locally raised, seasonal, and organic foods is to visit your local farmers' market or food co-op, and shop according to the season. Your community may have a Community Supported Agriculture (CSA) program, in which local farmers deliver a weekly box of produce for a set fee. This is a great way to support local farmers.

GRILLED YELLOWTAIL TUNA
ON ASIAN EDAMAME BEAN SALAD

❋ SERVES 6 ❋

Any type of firm fish tastes delicious marinated in a lightly spicy dressing, seared and served perched on a color-ful, crunchy salad of sprouts and bright green edamame (fresh soybeans). Bluefin and yellowfin tuna are being hunted to near-extinction all over the world, so please choose other types of similar fish (see "Sustainable Fish," opposite) such as fresh American-caught yellowtail or albacore, or buy a fish that is pole-caught locally. The fish should be served warm from the pan on the chilled salad.

Fish should always be impeccably fresh. At the store, fish should be displayed on, or better still, in clean crushed ice. Fish filets should smell fresh; whole fish should look shiny and plump. Once you get the fish home, set it in a colander over a bowl, top with a plastic bag of ice, and use as soon as possible. Be sure to wash your hands both before and after handling the fish.

1 1/2 POUNDS FRESH YELLOWTAIL OR ALBACORE, CUT INTO 6 PIECES

GREEN CURRY–CILANTRO SAUCE (RECIPE FOLLOWS)

2 CUPS COOKED SHELLED EDAMAME

2 CUPS MUNG BEAN SPROUTS

1 SMALL CARROT, PEELED AND GRATED

1/2 CUCUMBER, PEELED AND THINLY SLICED

1/4 CUP SLICED GREEN ONIONS

2 CUPS SPICY BABY GREENS, SUCH AS MUSTARD GREENS, TATSOI, MIZUNA, ARUGULA, OR CRESS

1/4 RED BELL PEPPER, CUT INTO THIN STRIPS

6 LEAVES RED LETTUCE OR BUTTER LETTUCE

1 TABLESPOON SESAME SEEDS

1. Marinate the fish in 1/2 cup of the sauce for 30 minutes.

2. In a large bowl, combine the edamame with 1/2 cup dressing. Add the sprouts, carrot, cucumber, onions, baby greens, and red pepper.

3. Preheat a grill or grill pan on high heat. Sear the fish on both sides to desired doneness—about 1 minute per side for rare, 2 minutes for medium-rare.

4. Set a lettuce leaf on each plate and top with 1/3 cup of the salad.

5. Cut the fish into thin slices and fan over the salad. Sprinkle 1/2 teaspoon sesame seeds over each serving of fish. Serve with additional sauce on the side.

VARIATION
✦ Substitute lightly cooked fresh green peas for the edamame.

GREEN CURRY–CILANTRO SAUCE

✴ MAKES 3 CUPS ✴

This sauce is so good you could eat it with a spoon. Try it as a salad dressing, as a dip with raw vegetables, or drizzled on fish. For a spicier sauce, add more of the curry paste. Both the Thai curry paste and sweet chile sauce are available at Asian markets.

4 CLOVES GARLIC, PEELED

2-INCH PIECE FRESH GINGER, PEELED AND CHOPPED

1/2 CUP SOY SAUCE

1/2 CUP MIRIN (SWEET RICE WINE)

1/2 CUP RED WINE VINEGAR

1/2 CUP AGAVE SYRUP OR MAPLE SYRUP

2 TO 4 TABLESPOONS THAI GREEN CURRY PASTE

1/2 CUP NATURAL PEANUT BUTTER

1 TEASPOON THAI SWEET CHILE SAUCE

1 BUNCH FRESH CILANTRO, STEMMED AND CHOPPED (ABOUT 3/4 CUP)

In a blender, combine all ingredients except the cilantro. Puree until smooth, then stir in the cilantro.

VARIATION
✦ The Thai green curry paste in the sauce is mildly spicy. Indian curry powder may be substituted.

SUSTAINABLE FISH

Do you love to eat fish and seafood? Many desirable fish—tuna, swordfish, Chilean sea bass—as well as most coastal species are in steep decline, hunted to extinction by unregulated and predatory fishing practices, or destroyed by pollution. If we as consumers do not act responsibly, our fish populations will soon collapse. If you care about our oceans and having safe fish, please choose sustainable species and don't buy endangered fish. Go to the Monterrey Bay Aquarium website (mbayaq.org) and click on Seafood Watch, where the complicated issue is laid out clearly. There's even a printable guide listing fish as green (OK to eat), yellow (use caution), and red (avoid) that may be taken to markets and restaurants. Another excellent resource is the Marine Stewardship Council (msc.org), an international non-profit organization certifies sustainable fisheries around the globe.

MSC-certified sustainable fisheries are carefully managed and monitored by local governments. American sustainable fisheries include American caught and packed king crab, halibut, black cod, Dungeness crab, and many others. Seafood products from Asia and Russia should be avoided.

SUMMER 🌿 81

GUAVA CRÈME BRÛLÉE

❋ MAKES SIX 4-OUNCE SERVINGS ❋

The gorgeous perfume of guava fills Mexico's summer markets; look for them in Asian or Latin supermarkets. Choose super ripe guavas that you can smell. The skins may be imperfect, but it's what's inside that counts: little bits of pink fruit that will give this light crème brûlée the sweet taste of the tropics.

A brûléed crust requires a small amount of sugar and a butane torch, which is available at gourmet cookware stores. (Professional cooks use small propane torches.) Do not try to caramelize the sugar under a broiler. The low fat content makes the crème prone to curdling. The custard is also satisfying without any sugar crust.

1½ CUPS MILK

ZEST OF 1 ORANGE

3 WHOLE EGGS

2 EGG YOLKS

½ CUP PACKED DARK BROWN SUGAR

2 TABLESPOONS VANILLA EXTRACT

3 LARGE OR 6 SMALL VERY RIPE GUAVAS, PEELED, SEEDED, COARSELY CHOPPED, AND DRAINED, OR ⅓ CUP PINK GUAVA PUREE (SEE NOTE)

1 TABLESPOON GRANULATED WHITE SUGAR OR RAW CANE SUGAR (DEMERARA SUGAR)

1. Preheat the oven to 350 degrees F.

2. Pour the milk into a 2-quart heavy-bottomed saucepan. Add the orange zest and heat over medium heat until very hot, with bubbles forming around the edge of the pan, but not boiling. Remove from heat and let stand 5 minutes.

3. Break the eggs into a mixing bowl, add the yolks, brown sugar, and the vanilla, and mix thoroughly. Slowly add about a third of the hot milk to the eggs, whisking as you pour; this tempers the eggs. Whisk in the rest of the hot milk a little at a time. You now have a custard.

4. Strain the custard back into the pan through a fine-mesh sieve, and carefully skim off any foam from the top.

5. Spread a tablespoon of chopped guava or guava puree on the bottom of each of six 6-ounce ramekins or custard cups. Divide the custard evenly among the ramekins.

6. Place the ramekins in a rectangular baking pan with high sides and carefully pour 1 inch of boiling water into the pan. Cover with foil and bake on the middle rack of the oven for approximately 30 minutes, or until the custards are no longer jiggly in the centers.

7. Remove from the oven, take off the foil, and let the custards cool in the water. Once they are cool, remove from the pan, cover, and refrigerate for up to 48 hours.

8. Just before serving, pat the tops of the custards dry with a paper towel. Top each serving with ½ teaspoon granulated sugar, tapping and tipping the ramekin to evenly coat the surface. Caramelize the sugar with a small butane or propane torch by holding the flame about 1 inch from the surface and moving it slowly back and forth. The sugar will first melt, then brown. Serve immediately.

NOTE: Look for frozen guava puree in Asian, Cuban, Mexican, or Puerto Rican markets.

VARIATION

✦ Any fresh fruit, in small pieces, may be used in place of the guava. Fresh locally grown berries, especially raspberries or blueberries, or well-drained orange or grapefruit segments, are especially good surprises.

Baja Fish Tacos

✦

CORN, CILANTRO, AND ARUGULA SALAD WITH YOGURT DRESSING

BAJA FISH TACOS WITH SALSA BAR

BLACK BEANS WITH EPAZOTE

LEMON VERBENA RICE PUDDING WITH FRESH FRUIT AND PISTACHIOS

✦

Party time! For a summer fiesta, nothing beats Baja-style fish tacos, complete with a full salsa bar. Here are some of the Ranch's best-loved recipes, including Deborah Szekely's famous Aztec Guacamole. A fresh corn salad, black beans, and lemon verbena-infused rice pudding (arroz con leche) are delicious twists on Mexican classics. Nearly the whole menu can be made well ahead of time, including the salsas and beans. All that remains to be done as guests arrive is to cook the fish and heat the tortillas. All the recipes in this menu may be doubled or tripled to serve a crowd.

CORN, CILANTRO, AND ARUGULA SALAD WITH YOGURT DRESSING

❋ SERVES 6 ❋

Here, the combination of cilantro in two forms—fresh green leaves and crushed seeds (called coriander), which have a distinct flavor of their own—is a perfect example of the dimensions of taste that Jesús teaches his students. This colorful salad is a burst of Mexican tastes using all Tres Estrellas' summer stars: barely cooked sweet corn, waves of dark green, peppery arugula leaves to wake up your taste buds, and a tangy, creamy dressing. Red radishes add color. Look for unusual radish varieties like lovely pink and green watermelon radishes.

4 TO 5 EARS LARGE SWEET CORN, SHUCKED AND SILK REMOVED

1 TABLESPOON OLIVE OIL

4 CUPS BABY ARUGULA, STEMMED

12 LARGE RADISHES, THINLY SLICED

1 TEASPOON CORIANDER SEEDS, CRUSHED

2 TABLESPOONS CHOPPED FRESH CILANTRO

YOGURT DRESSING

¼ CUP YOGURT

¼ CUP WHITE WINE VINEGAR OR CIDER VINEGAR

1 TABLESPOON DIJON MUSTARD

¼ TEASPOON SEA SALT, OR TO TASTE

1½ TABLESPOONS OLIVE OIL

¼ TO ½ TEASPOON GROUND CHIPOTLE (OPTIONAL)

1. With a sharp knife, cut all the kernels from the cobs. You should have about 4 cups.

2. In a 10-inch sauté pan, heat 1 tablespoon olive oil over medium-high heat. Add the corn, cover, and sauté 2 to 5 minutes, until tender. Set aside to cool.

3. In a large bowl, mix the corn, arugula, radishes, coriander, and cilantro. Cover and chill for 1 hour.

4. In a small bowl, whisk together the yogurt, vinegar, mustard, and salt until well blended. Gradually whisk in the remaining 1½ tablespoons of oil until emulsified, and add the chipotle, if desired. The dressing may be made ahead of time and refrigerated for up to 1 hour.

5. Just before serving, toss the salad with half the dressing. Add more dressing to taste.

NOTE: Cilantro bolts (flowers) quickly in the heat, so you can easily harvest and dry your own fresh coriander seed.

CORN

Corn is the "mother" of Mexico—the foundation of their ancient culture, unique cuisine, and glorious mythology. More than 300 distinct varieties of corn have been identified in Mexico alone. *Teozintle*, the wild maize from which all corn evolved, still grows in parts of the country.

While corn is most often eaten in the form of corn tortillas (made with nothing more than ground dried corn, lime, and water), fresh corn finds its way into traditional soups and *pastels* (casseroles). A favorite street food is corn on the cob grilled over charcoal with a squeeze of lime and a dusting of chile powder, or cut from the cob and tossed with mayonnaise and cotija cheese. The Ranch's chefs roast, pan-sear, or grill corn until it is smoky and chewy, then use the cooked corn for chiles rellenos stuffing, delicious soups, and pureed sauces, or toss the tender kernels into salads.

BAJA FISH TACOS WITH SALSA BAR

✺ MAKES 12 TACOS ✺

The port city of Ensenada lies on the Pacific coast, just an hour away from Rancho La Puerta. It is an historic fishing town with a bustling commercial fish market and many famous fish taco stands. This oven-baked version is a lighter variation of the legendary Ensenada fish taco (which is deep-fried in a crunchy beer batter), but it is equally delicious. Choose a firm fish that will hold its shape; anything from catfish to wild salmon works, or substitute shrimp. Note that an authentic Ensenada fish taco must be made with corn, not flour, tortillas, and shredded cabbage, not lettuce. Have a few extra tortillas on hand in case you have some extra filling.

1½ POUNDS BONELESS WHITE FISH, SUCH AS MAHI MAHI, RED SNAPPER, OR HALIBUT

1 CLOVE GARLIC, MINCED

1 SHALLOT, MINCED

1 TABLESPOON FRESH LIME OR LEMON JUICE

1 TEASPOON DRIED MEXICAN OREGANO

1 TEASPOON SEA SALT

½ TEASPOON FRESH GROUND BLACK PEPPER

1 TEASPOON OLIVE OIL

12 FRESH CORN TORTILLAS

1 CUP FINELY SHREDDED GREEN CABBAGE

CHIPOTLE LIME SAUCE (RECIPE FOLLOWS)

PICO DE GALLO (RECIPE FOLLOWS)

AZTEC GUACAMOLE (RECIPE FOLLOWS)

PICANTE SAUCE (RECIPE FOLLOWS)

MANGO SALSA (RECIPE FOLLOWS)

ANCHO CHILE SALSA (PAGE 39)

CUCUMBER-JICAMA SALSA (PAGE 149)

LIME WEDGES

1. Cut the fish into 12 pieces about 3 inches long and ¾ inch wide.

2. Place the fish in a baking dish with the garlic, shallot, lime juice, oregano, salt, and pepper. Toss gently to coat the fish. Cover and marinate fish for about an hour in refrigerator.

3. Preheat the oven to 375 degrees F. Brush a baking sheet lightly with the olive oil. Place fish pieces on a sheet pan and bake for about 15 minutes, or until firm.

4. Warm the tortillas on a flat grill and keep warm in a clean napkin in a tortilla warmer, or wrapped in foil in a warm oven until ready to serve.

5. Place a portion of fish in each warmed tortilla.

6. Top with 1 tablespoon shredded cabbage and 1 teaspoon of Chipotle Lime Sauce. Invite guests to fix their taco at the salsa bar, where you can serve the pico de gallo, guacamole, picante sauce, salsas, and lime wedges buffet style.

A HEALTHY COOKING SPRAY

For oiling sauté pans, preparing baking sheets or phyllo, or any of a thousand other uses, try using a refillable spray bottle (available at any hardware store) filled with olive oil. This works just as well as expensive cooking sprays. It is ecologically sound and inexpensive.

CHIPOTLE LIME SAUCE

No fish taco is complete without a squeeze of "secret sauce"—a lime-spiked cream that perfectly sets off all the other flavors. This version adds roasted red pepper and smoky-hot chipotle chiles. If you don't like spicy foods, leave the chipotle out.

Chipotles are red-ripe jalapeños that have been dried slowly over a wood fire. They have a subtle, smoky heat that can be addictive. Chipotles are a dull leathery brown color, easy to spot in the market among piles of sleek, shiny chiles. Jesús generally uses small pinches of dried ground chipotles to add a smoky flavor with very little heat. If you like spicy foods, try canned chipotle chiles in adobo, cooked with vinegar, garlic, tomato, and salt into a soft paste that is spicy and tart all at once. Use sparingly to add zip to salsa, dressings, stews, and sauces.

¹/₄ CUP PUREED ROASTED RED PEPPER (SEE PAGE 108)

3 TABLESPOONS ORGANIC OLIVE-OIL MAYONNAISE

1 TABLESPOON FINELY CHOPPED CANNED CHIPOTLES IN ADOBO (OPTIONAL)

2 TEASPOONS FRESH LIME JUICE

Combine all the ingredients, cover, and refrigerate until ready to serve.

PICO DE GALLO

Pico de Gallo is the classic Mexican table salsa, rich with tomatoes, onions, cilantro, and the nip of chiles and fresh lime juice. You may adjust the proportions of tomatoes and other ingredients to your liking, or leave the chiles out altogether for a mild salsa fresca, but great tomatoes are a must. Be sure to season the salsa assertively with lime juice to get a great burst of flavor.

4 LARGE ROMA TOMATOES, SEEDED AND CUT INTO ¹/₄-INCH DICE

1 SMALL JALAPEÑO OR SERRANO CHILE, SEEDED AND MINCED (OPTIONAL)

¹/₂ CUP FINELY DICED WHITE OR RED ONION

3 TABLESPOONS CHOPPED FRESH CILANTRO

2 TABLESPOONS FRESH LIME JUICE, OR MORE TO TASTE

¹/₈ TEASPOON SEA SALT, OR TO TASTE

Combine all the ingredients and let the salsa stand for 30 minutes before serving.

AZTEC GUACAMOLE

❈ MAKES 2 CUPS ❈

This terrific guacamole is probably the Ranch's most enduringly popular recipe. Adding green vegetables to the avocado boosts the nutritional value of the guacamole and reduces the fat content. Most importantly, it tastes great.

If you are not using it to top tacos, serve with an assortment of raw vegetables and *tostaditas* (see page 149).

1 CUP FROZEN PEAS, SLIGHTLY THAWED

1 MEDIUM HASS AVOCADO, PEELED AND PITTED

2 TABLESPOONS FRESH LIME OR LEMON JUICE, OR TO TASTE

1 MEDIUM TOMATO, SEEDED AND CUT INTO ¼-INCH DICE

½ RED OR SWEET ONION, CUT INTO ⅛-INCH DICE

1 JALAPEÑO OR SERRANO CHILE, SEEDED AND MINCED

3 TABLESPOONS CHOPPED FRESH CILANTRO

1 TEASPOON MINCED FRESH GARLIC

½ TEASPOON SEA SALT

¼ TEASPOON FRESH GROUND BLACK PEPPER

1. In a blender or in the bowl of a food processor, process the peas until smooth.

2. In a medium bowl, mash the avocado with a fork or potato masher.

Add the juice, tomato, onion, jalapeño, cilantro, garlic, salt, and black pepper. Add the peas and mix well.

3. If the guacamole won't be served immediately, press a piece of plastic wrap directly onto the surface to prevent browning.

VARIATION

✦ Instead of peas, use 1 cup of well-cooked broccoli, edamame, or cooked asparagus tips.

PICANTE SAUCE

≋ MAKES ¾ CUP ≋

Warning: Hot! This salsa is made with chiles de arbol, long thin dried red chiles with a ferocious kick. Even chile lovers should use very small drops.

10 DRIED CHILES DE ARBOL, SEEDED

½ CUP HOT WATER

1 ROMA TOMATO, CORED AND CUT INTO SEVERAL PIECES

1 SMALL CLOVE GARLIC, PEELED

1 TEASPOON WHITE VINEGAR

½ TEASPOON SALT, OR TO TASTE

1. Break the chiles into small pieces and soak in the hot water for about 30 minutes, covered. Place the chiles and their soaking liquid in a blender and puree until smooth.

2. Add the vinegar, garlic, tomato, and salt, and pulse until smooth, adding more water as necessary, 1 tablespoon at a time, to make a thin sauce. Strain if desired. Taste for seasoning.

MANGO SALSA

≋ MAKES 2 CUPS ≋

A nontraditional combination of typical flavors, this salsa is also good on grilled fish or as a dressing on a mixed green salad, on *tostaditas* (page 149) or Shrimp Enchiladas with Picante Sauce (page 150).

½ CUP DICED RED ONION

1 ROMA TOMATO, SEEDED AND CUT INTO ¼-INCH DICE

¼ CUP CILANTRO LEAVES, CHOPPED

¼ JALAPEÑO OR SERRANO CHILE, SEEDED AND MINCED

1 TEASPOON SEA SALT

4 TABLESPOONS FRESH LIME JUICE (ABOUT 2 LIMES), OR TO TASTE

1 MANGO, PEELED, SEEDED, AND CUT INTO ½-INCH DICE

Combine all the ingredients in a serving bowl, stirring the mango in last.

VARIATION

✦ Add 1 tablespoon of drained capers and ¼ teaspoon fresh ground black pepper.

BLACK BEANS WITH EPAZOTE

Black beans are often cooked with a sprig of epazote, a fast-growing native herb that grows wild throughout the southwestern United States and in Mexico. It has a distinctive taste somewhere between mint and oregano. Epazote is available fresh in season or dried year-round in Latin and Mexican markets.

1 CUP DRIED BLACK BEANS, RINSED AND PICKED OVER

5 CUPS WATER

½ TEASPOON SALT

1 STALK FRESH EPAZOTE, OR ¼ TEASPOON DRIED

1 BAY LEAF

½ STALK CELERY

1 TABLESPOON OLIVE OIL

½ SMALL ONION, CUT INTO ½-INCH DICE

1 CLOVE GARLIC, MINCED

½ JALAPEÑO, SEEDED AND MINCED

¼ TEASPOON FRESH GROUND BLACK PEPPER

1. Combine beans, water, salt, epazote, bay leaf, and celery stalk in a 4-quart saucepan. Bring to a boil, then simmer over low heat for about 2 hours, or until the beans are very tender, making sure the beans are covered by liquid the whole time. (The beans may be made ahead of time up to this point and cooled, in their cooking liquid, and refrigerated.)

2. In a small sauté pan, heat the oil over medium heat. Add the onion, garlic, and jalapeño, and cook until softened, then add them to the beans, along with the black pepper. Simmer the beans for 30 minutes.

LEMON VERBENA RICE PUDDING WITH FRESH FRUIT AND PISTACHIOS

❧ SERVES 6 TO 8 ❧

Arroz con leche is a favorite Mexican dessert, traditionally made with thick, sweetened condensed milk and cinnamon. In this recipe, rice is infused with the luscious flavor of lemon verbena and gently folded into a lightened-up cream. Top each serving of the pudding with whatever fresh fruit is ripe and in season. A scattering of bright green pistachio nuts (which grow at Tres Estrellas) adds crunch and color. For a party, you could serve very small portions in pretty glasses on a buffet.

2 CUPS MILK

1 1/2 CUPS WATER

2 TABLESPOONS CHOPPED LEMON VERBENA LEAVES

1 CUP LONG-GRAIN BROWN RICE

1 CINNAMON STICK

1/2 CUP RICOTTA CHEESE

1 TEASPOON VANILLA EXTRACT

1/2 CUP AGAVE SYRUP OR MAPLE SYRUP, OR TO TASTE

1/4 TEASPOON GROUND CINNAMON

2 CUPS FRESH FRUIT

1/4 CUP PISTACHIO NUTS, CRUSHED OR CHOPPED

6 TO 8 FRESH LEMON VERBENA, LEMON BALM, OR MINT SPRIGS (OPTIONAL)

1. In a small saucepan, combine 1 cup of the milk with the water. Bring to a simmer over medium heat and stir in the lemon verbena. Turn off the heat and let stand for 30 minutes, then strain out the leaves, returning the milk to the saucepan.

2. Add the rice and cinnamon stick, bring to a simmer, then reduce the heat to low. Cover and cook slowly for 15 minutes, or until the rice is soft. Remove the cinnamon stick.

3. In a blender, combine the remaining 1 cup milk, the ricotta cheese, vanilla, and syrup. Puree completely, then stir into the cooked rice along with the ground cinnamon.

4. Half-fill parfait glasses with rice pudding. Spoon some fresh fruit on top and garnish with a pinch of bright green pistachios and an herb sprig, if desired.

LEMONY HERBS

When citrus is out of season, how do you get that lemony zing? Lemon verbena is one alternative. Lemon verbena is not really an herb, but a medium-sized flowering bush whose leaves smell and taste pungently of mildly bitter citrus and resin. Other sources of citrus flavor include lemongrass, lemon balm, and kaffir lime leaves.

" THOSE WHO ARE ONE IN FOOD
ARE ONE IN LIFE. "
MALAGASY SAYING

Every region has its seasons. At the Ranch, there are no showy deciduous trees changing color or hard frosts to tell when the season has finally slipped from summer to fall. The fall air is as dry as stone and perfectly clear. From the top of the mountain, you can almost see the sparkle of the Pacific. Cold nights melt into cool, crisp mornings and warm afternoons. Leaves dry and wither away, leaving brilliant peppers stripped of their greenery and blazing red and orange down the garden rows. Golden quince and persimmons hang ready on the trees, and "tepee" stalks of dry corn stand in the field. The very last burst of late summer's tender herbs and fruit share the garden with hard-shelled squash and root vegetables that will be sturdy enough to last through the winter. ✦ Fall is the busiest season for everyone associated with the garden. The year's bounty must be harvested, stored, and preserved to see the kitchen through the slim pickings of the winter to come, so not a bit is wasted.

FALL
The Gift

Mountains of hard squash and potatoes are trundled into the root cellar, which smells powerfully of the curing garlic that wreaths the beams. The last tomatoes are torn up and sent to the dehydrator, making room for fall's crop of romaine, endive, bok choy, and kale. Long *ristras* of bright red peppers dangle from the rafters of the storehouse attic. Precious fennel flowers dry upside down over fine mesh, until the pollen can be gently shaken loose. A worker patiently strips the leaves from bags of dried herbs, sifts them through a screen, bags, and labels them: lemon thyme, sage, marjoram, oregano. Bags of fresh coriander seed and fennel seed are cracked open to let the last bits of moisture evaporate in the dry, cool air. The Ranch's stillroom, where essential oils and herb blends are made, is packed with jars of dried flowers and medicinal herbs. All is ready for winter.

Fall Colors

✴

CARROT AND GINGER SOUP WITH PEARS

HEIRLOOM APPLE AND SMOKED GOUDA SALAD
WITH WALNUT HONEY DRESSING

EXOTIC MUSHROOM AND SPINACH BEGGARS' PURSES IN PHYLLO

DESSERT DUET:
ROASTED BANANA–RUM SORBET *AND*
BANANAS FLAMBÉ WITH CHOCOLATE AND PISTACHIOS

✴

Fall brings a different breeze, a different feeling in the air. When your farmers' market is heaped with all the colors of fall, it's time to come inside and do some serious cooking. Make a soul-warming soup, try an heirloom apple, or indulge in the season's first nuts. Make playful phyllo "gifts" of mushrooms and spinach and, if you dare, a flambéed dessert.

CARROT AND GINGER SOUP WITH PEARS

❋ SERVES 6 ❋

Tres Estrellas' carrots are the best you will ever taste, right out of the ground. Their color and texture are enhanced in this soup by the first butternut squash off the vines that have been sprawling all summer. Though the carrots themselves are naturally sweet, an apple and a final garnish of pear balances the heat of the ginger. Jesús makes a point of slowly sautéing the carrots and onions to release the natural sugars.

2 TEASPOONS OLIVE OIL

4 MEDIUM CARROTS, PEELED AND ROUGHLY CHOPPED (ABOUT 2 CUPS)

1 SMALL WHITE ONION, PEELED AND ROUGHLY CHOPPED

1 CLOVE GARLIC, PEELED AND MINCED

3 TABLESPOONS PEELED, MINCED FRESH GINGER (SEE NOTE)

1 CUP PEELED, CUBED BUTTERNUT SQUASH

1 APPLE, PEELED, CORED, AND DICED

4 1/2 CUPS BASIC VEGETABLE STOCK (PAGE 176) OR WATER

1 1/2 TEASPOONS SEA SALT, OR TO TASTE

12-OUNCE CAN COCONUT MILK, OR 1 1/2 CUPS MILK

1 PEAR, PEELED, CORED, AND CUT INTO 1/2-INCH DICE

SLICED CHIVES

1. In a 2-quart stockpot, heat the olive oil over medium heat. Sauté the carrots and onion, and cook for several minutes, stirring often, until softened. Add the garlic, ginger, squash, and apple. Sauté until the garlic and ginger are fragrant.

2. Add the stock and salt. Reduce the heat to medium-low and simmer, covered, for 45 minutes, or until the vegetables are very tender.

3. In blender or in the bowl of a food processor, puree the soup until smooth. Add the coconut milk and taste, then add salt to taste. Reheat before serving.

4. Serve the soup very hot in warmed soup bowls with some diced pear and a sprinkling of chives.

NOTE: To peel ginger, scrape off the skin with a spoon.

VARIATIONS

✦ Set off the soup's beautiful color with a combination of green onion tops and fresh chopped parsley or cilantro.

✦ Toast whole-wheat bread, cut into croutons, and float a few in each bowl.

HEIRLOOM APPLE AND SMOKED GOUDA SALAD WITH HONEY WALNUT DRESSING

❀ SERVES 6 ❀

Fall and winter are cold enough in the Tecate mountains to keep apple trees happy, which is very chilly indeed. Heirloom apples are usually firm and tart, with lots of character. Any variety would be great on this perfect fall salad, with crisp apples, nuts, and smoky cheese mixed in with spiky, mildly bitter frisée and crimson radicchio.

1 LARGE HEAD CURLY ENDIVE (FRISÉE)

1/2 CUP FINELY SHREDDED RADICCHIO

2 LARGE SHALLOTS, MINCED

3 TABLESPOONS WALNUT OIL (SEE NOTE)

3 TABLESPOONS RICE VINEGAR

2 TABLESPOONS RED WINE VINEGAR

2 TABLESPOONS HONEY

1/2 TEASPOON FRESH GROUND BLACK PEPPER, OR MORE TO TASTE

2 LARGE, FIRM, TART APPLES, SUCH AS ANNA OR GRANNY SMITH, CORED, SLICED, AND CUT INTO JULIENNE

3/4 CUP WALNUTS, TOASTED AND BROKEN INTO PIECES

3 OUNCES NATURAL SMOKED GOUDA OR SMOKED MOZZARELLA, CUT INTO 1/2-INCH CUBES

1/4 CUP GOLDEN RAISINS OR DRIED CHERRIES

1. Trim any tough, dark green leaves from the frisée. Break the head into leaves, wash well, and spin dry. Separate the curly frizz from the thick stems and tear the frizz into bite-sized pieces. Combine with the shredded radicchio and set aside.

2. In a blender, combine the shallots, oil, vinegars, honey, and pepper. Taste for seasoning and add pepper if needed.

3. Toss the greens with a small amount of dressing and divide among 6 chilled plates. Top each salad with some apples, walnuts, cheese, and raisins. Drizzle with additional dressing and serve immediately.

NOTE: Walnut oil may be found at specialty or gourmet shops. Buy only a small amount and keep it refrigerated. Nut oils are always used as an accent flavor, never for cooking. If the walnut oil is mild-flavored, you may want to add a little more than the amount called for in the recipe. A very fruity extra-virgin olive oil is a good substitute.

VARIATION

✦ Scatter golden yellow and orange flower petals from unsprayed fall flowers, such as marigolds, calendula, or mums, over the finished salad just before serving.

EXOTIC MUSHROOM AND SPINACH BEGGARS' PURSES IN PHYLLO

❊ SERVES 6 ❊

Tie each purse like a gift with a ribbon of green, and a fresh, edible flower. Mushrooms are a gift: delicious and packed with antioxidants. For the filling, use a variety of exotic mushrooms, such as shiitake, oyster, portobello, and cremini. The filling may be made a day ahead.

The purses are very quick to make with versatile phyllo leaves, found in the freezer section of most supermarkets. Spraying the purses with a small amount of oil helps the phyllo bake up crisp and brown. Use a refillable household spray bottle of oil rather than expensive cooking spray.

2 TEASPOONS OLIVE OIL, PLUS MORE TO SPRAY THE PHYLLO

1/2 MEDIUM WHITE ONION, PEELED AND CUT INTO 1/4-INCH DICE

1 CLOVE GARLIC, PEELED AND MINCED

4 OUNCES FRESH EXOTIC MUSHROOMS, SUCH AS OYSTER OR SHIITAKE, STEMMED AND ROUGHLY CHOPPED (ABOUT 2 CUPS)

1 POUND FRESH SPINACH LEAVES

6 BASIL LEAVES, FINELY CHOPPED

1 TABLESPOON CHOPPED FRESH DILL

1 TEASPOON SEA SALT, OR TO TASTE

1/4 TEASPOON FRESH GROUND BLACK PEPPER, OR TO TASTE

1/4 TEASPOON CAYENNE PEPPER

1/8 TEASPOON FRESH GRATED NUTMEG

1/2 CUP RICOTTA CHEESE

1/4 CUP CRUMBLED FETA

1/4 CUP GRATED MOZZARELLA CHEESE

1 EXTRA-LARGE EGG, BEATEN

1 PACKAGE PHYLLO DOUGH, THAWED ACCORDING TO PACKAGE DIRECTIONS

LONG CHIVE STEMS WITH FLOWERS, OR GREEN ONION TOPS, CUT INTO LONG "TIES," AND SMALL FLOWERS WITH STEMS (OPTIONAL)

1. In a 10-inch sauté pan, heat 1 teaspoon of the olive oil over medium heat. Add the onion and garlic and cook, stirring often, for 2 minutes, or until soft.

2. Add the mushrooms and continue to cook, stirring until they are soft. Scrape the mushrooms into a small mixing bowl and return the pan to the heat.

3. Add the remaining 1 teaspoon olive oil to the pan and cook the spinach until just wilted. Cool, drain, finely chop the spinach, and add it to the mushrooms. Add the basil, dill, salt, black pepper, cayenne, and nutmeg, and stir to combine thoroughly. Taste and adjust seasoning with additional salt and pepper, if needed.

4. In a small bowl, combine the ricotta, feta, and mozzarella cheeses with the beaten egg, then add to the mushrooms and spinach. (The recipe may be made ahead to this point, and refrigerated for up to 24 hours. Drain thoroughly in a large sieve before proceeding.)

5. Preheat the oven to 350 degrees F.

6. Read the package directions on phyllo dough. Unfold the phyllo sheets. If they are full sheets, cut in half across the middle to make approximate 6-inch squares. Discard any cracked or broken sheets. (To prevent drying, always keep the phyllo covered with a dry kitchen towel when not in use). Set 1 square of phyllo on a baking sheet and spray lightly with olive oil. Set 2 squares of phyllo on top at an angle to the first, and spray the top sheet. Set another square of phyllo on the top at a different angle and

spray the top sheet. You should have 4 phyllo leaves in the stack. If the phyllo cracks at any point, add a patch.

7. Spoon ½ cup of filling into the center of the phyllo sheets. Gather up the corners of the phyllo like a kerchief and hold in one hand. Pinch the bundle just above the filling and squeeze gently. Give a little twist to make a purse. Repeat with the remaining phyllo and filling.

8. Bake the purses for 35 minutes, until the filling is very hot all the way through and the phyllo is crisp and brown. Serve within 15 minutes, or the bottoms will become soggy.

9. Just before serving, cut the flower from the chive, leaving a 2-inch stem. Pour hot tap water over the chives to soften them slightly, drain, and pat dry. Gently tie a chive around the neck of each purse and tuck in the flower. If using green onion tops, prepare them in the same way.

VARIATIONS

✦ Make tiny purses for a party, with 1 tablespoon of filling. (Tying with chives is up to you.)

✦ Make one big spanakopita by lining a large baking dish with several layers of oiled phyllo sheets. Spread the filling evenly over the top and finish with four more layers of oiled phyllo. Bake until crisp and well-browned, then cut into small squares to serve.

OLIVE OIL

Over the years, Ranch cooking has evolved into a Baja Mediterranean style based on whole grains, plenty of fresh fruits and vegetables, and small amounts of protein in the form of fish, all sparkling with vibrant Mexican flavors and plenty of ¡ole! Quality ingredients are at the heart of this kind of simple cooking, and Jesús uses mild, fruity Baja extra-virgin olive oils exclusively.

The extra-virgin olive oil used at the Ranch and La Cocina Que Canta is made nearby, from olives grown in the Valle de Guadalupe.

When you buy olive oil, choose American-grown extra-virgin oils, preferably organic, with 2 to 3 percent acidity. Think about olive oil as a seasoning. Do you like a fruity, mild oil or a peppery, strong oil? Perhaps you would like different oils for different uses. Color is no indicator of freshness, taste, or quality. Use your nose to choose a fruity, fresh-smelling oil.

Imported olive oils may be old or of uncertain lineage—some countries permit deceptive labeling. In any case, why buy an oil that may have logged thousands of miles and months on the shelf, when good American oils are readily available and reasonably priced?

DESSERT DUET

You've never tasted bananas quite like this. Roasted bananas are frozen into a creamy-textured, rum-tickled sorbet that melts onto ripe bananas sautéed with orange, and drizzled with chocolate and pistachios. Either element of the duet would be delicious on its own. Together, it is truly sumptuous. To serve them together, place a scoop of Roasted Banana–Rum Sorbet on the sautéed bananas, drizzle a little chocolate over the top, and garnish with the chopped pistachios.

ROASTED BANANA–RUM SORBET

❋ MAKES 3 CUPS ❋

DEBORAH REMEMBERS . . . *Wherever my family lived—Tahiti, Mexico, New York, California—during my childhood, we always had bananas at the ready. In Rio Corona, Mexico, they grew near the Professor's health camp in a big clump down at the bottom of a ravine. We really did pick our own. I can honestly say that I never had roasted banana sorbet as a child, but this recipe has become a favorite.*

There's no cream in this recipe, just the creamy smoothness of pure banana, which deepens when roasted. Sometimes the very simplest tastes are the best.

4 LARGE, RIPE BANANAS

⅓ CUP DARK MAPLE SYRUP

1 TABLESPOON DARK RUM OR VANILLA BEAN PASTE (OPTIONAL)

1. Preheat the oven to 350 degrees F. Roast the bananas in their skins, right on the oven rack, for 10 minutes, or until the skin is blackened. Peel the bananas over a bowl to catch all the juices.

2. In a blender, puree the bananas and their juices with the syrup and rum, if desired. Chill the puree in a covered container, then freeze in an ice cream maker according to the manufacturer's directions, or simply freeze in a covered container (see page 125)

NOTE: If the sorbet gets too hard to scoop, leave the container at room temperature for 30 minutes to soften.

VARIATION

✦ This recipe tastes great paired with Mayan Chocolate Sorbet (page 163), melting on a slice of grilled pineapple, or alongside roasted pears (see page 158).

BANANAS FLAMBÉ
WITH CHOCOLATE AND PISTACHIOS

❉ SERVES 6 ❉

This is fun to cook right at the table if you have a chafing dish and brave guests. The dish is very fast, so have all your ingredients ready before you turn on the heat.

2 TABLESPOONS MILK

1 TABLESPOON COINTREAU OR OTHER ORANGE-BASED LIQUEUR

3 OUNCES SEMISWEET CHOCOLATE, CHOPPED

2 LARGE RIPE BUT FIRM BANANAS

2 TABLESPOONS UNSALTED BUTTER

6 DRIED FIGS, STEMS REMOVED

2 TABLESPOONS BROWN SUGAR

ZEST OF 1 WASHED ORANGE

2 TABLESPOONS BRANDY

3 TABLESPOONS CHOPPED PISTACHIOS

1. In a small heatproof bowl, combine the milk and Cointreau, and set over a saucepan of simmering water. Stir until the chocolate is completely melted, then remove from heat.

2. Cut the bananas in half lengthwise and cut the halves into 6 equal pieces.

3. In a 10-inch sauté pan, melt the butter over medium heat. Lay the banana pieces, cut-side down, in the butter. Add the figs, brown sugar, and orange zest. Cook over medium heat until the bananas brown on one side.

4. Turn the bananas over and raise the heat to high. Remove the pan from the heat and pour the brandy over the bananas. Set the pan back on the heat and tilt the pan away from yourself so that it flames. If the brandy does not flame, the sauce will still taste fine. Continue to cook, shaking gently, until the flame dies, about 1 minute.

5. Divide the bananas and figs among 6 plates. Top with a scoop of Banana-Rum Sorbet and a sprinkling of toasted pistachios.

FALL GREENS

✦

CREAMY LIMA BEAN SOUP

POLENTA GRATIN WITH BRAISED FALL GREENS,
GOAT CHEESE, AND ROASTED BELL PEPPERS

QUINCE-APPLE MERMELADA TARTLETS

✦

Dark leafy greens stage a comeback in the cool fall weather. Here, they are quickly sautéed and piled on cheesy baked polenta with a side of roasted peppers. Greens also appear in one of Jesús' most popular soups, a creamy lima bean and herb soup. Finish with tarts featuring one of fall's treasures, the quince, slow-cooked into thick mermelada. Oven-roasted squash with a drizzle of honey (see Basics, page 165) would be a good accompaniment. This is the kind of dinner that vegetarians dream of.

CREAMY LIMA BEAN SOUP

✳ SERVES 6 ✳

Buttery lima beans are the base for a light soup finished with handfuls of fresh herbs, vitamin-rich greens, and a final swirl of creamy, tangy yogurt. For more about legumes and cooking techniques, see page 177.

1 CUP SMALL DRIED LIMA BEANS

4 CUPS WATER

6 CUPS BASIC VEGETABLE STOCK (PAGE 176) OR WATER

2 TEASPOONS SEA SALT

2 WHOLE CLOVES

1 MEDIUM ONION, PEELED

1 BAY LEAF

1 1/2 TEASPOONS OLIVE OIL

1/2 CUP SCALLIONS, GREEN PARTS ONLY

1 TABLESPOON MINCED GARLIC

1 1/2 CUPS CHARD, SPINACH, OR KALE, STEMMED AND SHREDDED

1/4 CUP FRESH FLAT-LEAF PARSLEY, CHOPPED

1/4 CUP FRESH TARRAGON LEAVES, CHOPPED

1 CUP YOGURT

1/2 TEASPOON FRESH GROUND BLACK PEPPER

1. Soak the beans in the water overnight.

2. Drain the beans and place them in a 3-quart stockpot with the stock and 1 teaspoon of sea salt and bring to a boil. Stick the cloves in the onion, using one to fasten the bay leaf to the onion, and add to the soup. Reduce the heat to low, cover, and simmer, stirring occasionally, until the beans are very tender, about 1 1/2 hours.

3. Remove the onion, cloves, and bay leaf. Puree half the soup in a blender and add it back to the soup.

4. In a small sauté pan, heat the oil over medium heat. Saute the scallions and garlic for 3 minutes, or until softened.

5. Just before serving, add the scallions and garlic, spinach, parsley, and tarragon to the soup.

6. Whisk the yogurt until smooth and add to the soup. Season with the remaining teaspoon of sea salt and pepper. Heat gently for several minutes, but do not boil.

VARIATIONS

✦ To make a beautiful pale green soup, puree the entire soup in a blender.

✦ Top with a few minced chives or toasted bread cut into croutons.

POLENTA GRATIN WITH BRAISED FALL GREENS, GOAT CHEESE, AND ROASTED BELL PEPPERS

❋ SERVES 6 ❋

There are both old- and new-world elements to this recipe. Polenta, a kind of thick, slow-cooked corn grits, is famously Italian—except the corn originated in Mexico, as did the peppers. Here, the polenta is a platform for sweet roasted bell peppers and slowly braised greens.

And what gorgeous greens they are. Tres Estrellas produces at least eight kinds of kale, as well as other varieties of flavorful, healthy greens: Swiss chard, collard greens, turnip or beet greens, spinach, Lacinato (Tuscan) kale, rapini, and broccolini.

4 ¼ CUPS WATER OR BASIC VEGETABLE STOCK (PAGE 176)

1 TEASPOON SEA SALT

1½ CUPS COARSE YELLOW CORNMEAL (POLENTA)

2 TABLESPOONS OLIVE OIL

¼ CUP FINE GRATED PARMESAN CHEESE

1 TABLESPOON CHOPPED FRESH THYME OR ROSEMARY LEAVES

1 LARGE BUNCH FALL GREENS, SUCH AS SWISS CHARD, COLLARD GREENS, AND KALE, STEMMED AND CUT INTO 1-INCH PIECES (ABOUT 6 CUPS)

½ SMALL WHITE ONION, PEELED AND CUT INTO ¼-INCH DICE

2 CLOVES GARLIC, PEELED AND MINCED

½ TEASPOON SEA SALT

3 ROASTED RED BELL PEPPERS (PAGE 108), PEELED, SEEDED, AND CUT INTO THIN STRIPS

2 OUNCES GOAT CHEESE, CRUMBLED (ABOUT ½ CUP)

TRES ESTRELLAS SALSA (PAGE 28)

1. Make the polenta at least 1 hour ahead of time. Bring 4 cups of the water to a boil, add the salt, and slowly whisk in the cornmeal. Cook, stirring constantly, until the mixture comes to a boil and thickens. Reduce the heat to low and cook for 30 minutes, stirring often. The polenta will be very thick.

2. Brush a 11 × 9-inch baking dish with some of the olive oil. Spread the polenta evenly into the dish. Sprinkle the Parmesan and herbs evenly over the surface of the hot polenta. Cool completely and chill, unwrapped, until firm.

3. Preheat the oven to 350 degrees F. Use a sharp knife to cut the polenta into 6 squares, then cut each square

diagonally to form 2 triangles. Lightly oil a large baking sheet, set the polenta triangles on it in rows, and bake for 30 minutes.

4. While the polenta is baking, wash the greens in several changes of water and drain thoroughly.

5. In a 10-inch sauté pan, heat the remaining olive oil over medium heat. Add the onion and garlic, and cook, stirring, for 2 minutes. Add the greens, season with the salt, and cook, stirring, for 1 minute, or until the greens start to wilt.

6. Add the remaining ¼ cup of water to the pan and cover. Reduce the heat to medium-low and cook for 10 minutes, or until the greens are quite soft. Keep warm.

7. Remove the polenta from the oven and transfer 2 triangles to each of 6 warmed plates. Lay several strips of roasted peppers on the polenta and set the greens on top. Crumble a little goat cheese over the peppers and greens. Return to the oven for 5 minutes, and then serve with warmed sauce on the side.

VARIATIONS

✦ Puree the roasted peppers with a small amount of vegetable stock to make a quick, easy sauce.

✦ Add sautéed mushrooms to the greens.

✦ Top with a few capers, or sprinkle with chopped fresh basil or chives.

✦ Substitute feta cheese or cotija cheese for the goat cheese.

ROASTED PEPPERS

Peppers take over the garden like an invasion of colorful hippies at a summer festival. Salvador grows mostly mild peppers, though they might be wildly individual in appearance and taste. Jesús points out that different shapes and colors from the same plant might taste sweeter or more herbal, because of how they ripened. Most peppers are used fresh in salads and *sofrito*, but long strings of mild, red

Nardello peppers bedeck the upper floor of the drying room. During the winter they will be ground or turned into salsa.

Peppers are always roasted whole, with stem and seeds intact. Roasting removes the thick skin from the pepper and develops and concentrates the flavor. To roast, cook them directly over a hot gas flame, on a hot grill or grill pan, under a hot broiler, or in a very hot, dry cast iron frying pan, turning occasionally until the skin is blistered and blackened on all sides. Roasting peppers in the oven will not develop much flavor and will probably overcook them. Once the skin is charred, the peppers should be allowed to steam in a paper bag. Remove the skin by rubbing it off, then remove the stem and seeds. Never wash a roasted pepper in water, or it will lose much of its flavor.

QUINCE-APPLE MERMELADA TARTLETS

❋ SERVES 6 ❋

Quince, "the golden apples of the sun," have long symbolized fertility, abundance, and wealth. The trees grow best in a Mediterranean climate and can produce for decades. Given their hardy nature, it's no surprise that quince trees flourish at Tres Estrellas.

Look for pale-gold quince in fall. Even when ripe, the fruit will be rock-hard and very tart. Mexicans eat raw quince thinly sliced, with a squeeze of lime and some salt. It is even better slowly cooked with apple and spices until it reaches the pale-pink sweetness of *mermelada*.

1 TEASPOON VEGETABLE OIL

2 GREEN APPLES, PEELED, CORED, AND CUT INTO 1/2-INCH DICE

1 QUINCE, PEELED, CORED, AND CUT INTO 1/2-INCH DICE

1/2 CUP DRIED CRANBERRIES

1/4 TEASPOON FRESH GRATED NUTMEG

1 CUP ORGANIC APPLE JUICE

ONE 2-INCH CINNAMON STICK

2 TABLESPOONS AGAVE SYRUP

6 TARTLET BASES (SEE PAGE 73)

WHIPPED CREAM

1. In a medium pan, heat the oil and sauté the apples and quince for 5 minutes.

2. Add the cranberries and nutmeg, and cook a few minutes more to soften.

3. Add the apple juice, cinnamon stick, and syrup. Reduce the heat and cook, stirring often, until the liquid evaporates, about 25 minutes.

4. Remove the cinnamon stick, put half of the mixture into the bowl a food processor, and puree. Stir the pureed mixture back into the remaining fruit.

5. Top each tartlet base with a dollop of *mermelada* and some whipped cream. Serve immediately. Refrigerate any leftover *mermelada*.

VARIATIONS

✦ Make with firm green apples alone, and cook only until tender and all the liquid has evaporated—about 15 minutes.

✦ Sprinkle the tartlets with chopped nuts, such as pistachios or almonds.

CINNAMON

All Mexican markets sell long quills of cinnamon bark tied into bundles with coarse twine. This is true cinnamon, also known as Ceylon cinnamon. The thin bark is crumbly and light in flavor. Jesús uses this type of cinnamon in both sweet and savory recipes to add color and a complexity of flavor. Founder Deborah is a big booster of cinnamon's antioxidant properties, and she uses it in many recipes. In folk medicine, cinnamon is used as an aphrodisiac and digestive aid.

What is sold as cinnamon is the United States is not cinnamon at all, but a bark called cassia. Cassia is thick, darker in color, and has a powerful, almost hot flavor.

FOR FRIENDS

✦

ROMAINE HEARTS AND ESCAROLE WITH KALAMATA OLIVES,
TOASTED PINE NUTS, AND CREAMY ASIAGO DRESSING

MEDITERRANEAN SAFFRON STEW WITH LEMON ZEST AIOLI

RANCHO LA PUERTA FLAXSEED BREAD

PEAR STRUDEL WITH BROWN SUGAR CREAM

✦

*Baby vegetables have their place. But grown-up vegetables, like old friends,
are more interesting—the kind you really want to spend time with.
At the Ranch, this Mediterranean stew would be loaded with full-flavored squash,
carrots, peppers, and potatoes; the pear strudel would be made from sweet
red pears from Tres Estrellas' orchard. This collection of casual recipes lets you
spend time with your friends instead of in the kitchen.*

ROMAINE HEARTS AND ESCAROLE WITH KALAMATA OLIVES, TOASTED PINE NUTS, AND CREAMY ASIAGO DRESSING

❋ SERVES 6 ❋

Romaine makes a comeback in fall, when temperatures cool off. Here it is combined with escarole, an unusual fall green that is pale green and faintly bitter. Choose a good-quality imported Asiago cheese (Jesús prefers it to Parmesan) for the dressing; some is used to thicken the dressing and the rest is tossed with the greens. Jesús uses very little oil in his dressings, preferring instead to thicken creamy dressings with tangy yogurt.

1 MEDIUM SHALLOT

2 CLOVES GARLIC, PEELED

1 CUP NONFAT YOGURT

2/3 CUP GRATED ASIAGO

2 TABLESPOONS EXTRA-VIRGIN OLIVE OIL

2 TABLESPOONS FRESH LIME JUICE

1 TABLESPOON CHOPPED FRESH OREGANO LEAVES

1 1/4 TEASPOONS FRESH GROUND BLACK PEPPER

1 TEASPOON SEA SALT, OR MORE TO TASTE

1/2 SMALL HEAD ROMAINE LETTUCE, OUTER LEAVES REMOVED, TOP 2 INCHES TRIMMED, AND CUT INTO 1-INCH PIECES

1/2 SMALL HEAD ESCAROLE, TRIMMED AND CUT INTO 1-INCH PIECES

1/2 SMALL HEAD RADICCHIO OR OTHER RED LETTUCE, TORN INTO 2-INCH PIECES

2 VINE-RIPENED TOMATOES, CUT INTO 1-INCH PIECES

3 GREEN ONIONS, CUT INTO 1/4-INCH DICE

1/2 CUP PITTED KALAMATA OLIVES

1/4 CUP TOASTED PINE NUTS

1. Combine the shallot, garlic, yogurt, 1/4 cup of the Asiago, olive oil, lime juice, oregano, pepper, and salt in a blender. Pulse until well combined. Refrigerate for at least 1 hour to allow the flavors to combine. The dressing is even better the next day.

2. Wash the lettuces, spin them dry, combine in a large bowl, and chill until ready to serve.

3. Just before serving, toss the greens, tomatoes, and green onions with half the dressing and the remaining cheese. Pass the rest of the dressing at the table. Divide the salad greens among 6 chilled plates. Set a few Kalamata olives on each salad, and scatter a few pine nuts on top.

VARIATIONS

✦ Substitute good Parmesan or Romano cheese for the Asiago.

✦ Vegans may use silken tofu instead of yogurt and omit the cheese.

MEDITERRANEAN SAFFRON STEW
WITH LEMON ZEST AIOLI

※ SERVES 6 ※

A steaming bowl of this hearty vegetable stew, radiant with real saffron, is just the thing on a chilly night. The aioli adds a shot of richness and pure garlic that lifts all the flavors to new heights.

The recipe is just a template for whatever marvelous collage of vegetables you choose. This time of year, gardens and farmers' markets are spilling over with tasty mature vegetables: cabbages, beets, onions, turnips, kohlrabi, squash, peppers, carrots, and parsnips. The hardest part will be deciding what to take home! Once you understand the process, use the recipe only as a guideline.

1 TABLESPOON EXTRA-VIRGIN OLIVE OIL

1 LARGE LEEK, WHITE PART ONLY, THINLY SLICED

1 TABLESPOON MINCED GARLIC

3 LARGE CARROTS, PEELED AND CUT INTO 1-INCH PIECES

1/2 MEDIUM YAM, PEELED AND CUT INTO 1-INCH PIECES

2 STALKS CELERY, TRIMMED AND CUT INTO 1/4-INCH DICE

2 MEDIUM ZUCCHINI, CUT INTO 1-INCH PIECES

1 LARGE TOMATO, CORED AND CHOPPED

1 MEDIUM GREEN OR YELLOW BELL PEPPER, SEEDED AND CUT INTO 1-INCH PIECES

4 TO 5 CUPS BASIC VEGETABLE STOCK (PAGE 176) OR WATER

1 CUP PUREED FRESH TOMATOES OR ORGANIC TOMATO SAUCE

1 TEASPOON SAFFRON THREADS

1/2 TEASPOON CRUSHED RED PEPPER

1 TEASPOON SEA SALT, OR TO TASTE

FRESH GROUND BLACK PEPPER

LEMON ZEST AIOLI

1 LARGE CLOVE GARLIC, PEELED

1/4 TEASPOON SEA SALT

3 TABLESPOONS ORGANIC OLIVE-OIL MAYONNAISE (SUCH AS HAIN'S)

1 TABLESPOON EXTRA-VIRGIN OLIVE OIL

2 TEASPOONS LEMON JUICE

1 TEASPOON FINELY GRATED LEMON ZEST

1 TABLESPOON CHOPPED BASIL, TARRAGON, OR OTHER FRESH HERB

1. In a large pot, heat the oil over medium heat. Gently sauté the leek for about 3 minutes, until softened. Add the minced garlic and stir for 1 minute. Add the carrots, yams, and celery, and continue to sauté for another 5 minutes, stirring occasionally. Add the zucchini, tomato, and bell pepper. Cover and cook for 3 minutes more.

2. Add the stock and the tomato sauce, and bring to a simmer. Reduce the heat to low, stir in the saffron and crushed pepper, cover, and continue cooking on low for about 30 minutes. Add salt and pepper to taste.

3. To make the lemon zest aioli, mash the garlic clove and salt with a fork to form a paste and mix with the mayonnaise. Add the olive oil, lemon juice, and zest, and mix until smooth. Stir in the herbs. Use within 24 hours.

4. Ladle stew into warmed bowls and serve hot with a dollop of aioli.

VARIATIONS

✦ Add a bunch of stemmed and shredded chard or kale for the last 10 minutes of cooking.

✦ Add 1 cup of firm tofu or tempeh, cut into small pieces, during the last 10 minutes of cooking.

RANCHO LA PUERTA FLAXSEED BREAD

❋ MAKES 2 SMALL LOAVES ❋

Great bread is almost a meal in itself. Best of all, when you bake your own bread, *you* control what's in it. Choose quality organic whole-grain flours and nuts, and you have bread the way it was meant to be—healthy, nourishing and delicious.

The dough can be made and kneaded by hand or in a mixer, with some small differences in texture. The recipe makes two small loaves. Rather than halving the recipe, make a full recipe and freeze one loaf. Note that the cracked wheat needs to be soaked overnight.

1 ½ CUPS WARM WATER

1 ½ TABLESPOONS ACTIVE DRY YEAST

¼ CUP EXTRA-VIRGIN OLIVE OIL

¼ CUP MOLASSES, MAPLE SYRUP OR HONEY

¼ CUP SUNFLOWER SEEDS

¼ CUP FLAX SEEDS

¼ CUP CRACKED WHEAT, SOAKED FOR 24 HOURS IN 1 CUP WATER

4 CUPS WHOLE-WHEAT FLOUR, PLUS MORE FOR KNEADING

1 TEASPOON SEA SALT

1. Place the warm water in a large mixing bowl. Sprinkle the yeast over the water and let it sit in a warm place until frothy, 5 to 8 minutes.

2. Add the oil, molasses, sunflower seeds, flax seeds, soaked cracked wheat, 2 cups of flour, and salt. Mix until well incorporated.

3. Stir in the remaining 2 cups of flour. Turn the dough out onto a floured board and knead until smooth and elastic, or knead with a standing mixer fitted with a dough hook attachment. Mix on low speed for 5 to 7 minutes, until the dough comes away completely from the sides of the bowl and is smooth and elastic.

4. Lightly oil a clean bowl and place the dough inside, turning once to coat. Cover with a damp tea towel and let the dough rise in a warm, draft-free place until it has doubled in bulk, 40 to 60 minutes.

5. Punch down the dough and divide into 2 equal portions. On a floured board, roll each piece of dough into a rectangle, approximately 8 inches long. Roll each rectangle into a loaf and pinch the edges together.

6. Place each loaf in an oiled small (about 6 inches long) loaf pan. Cover and let rise in a warm, draft-free place until the loaves have nearly doubled in bulk, about 45 minutes or longer.

7. Bake in a preheated 375-degree F oven for 40 to 60 minutes, or until the tops are browned and the loaves sound hollow when tapped. Remove from the pan and place on a rack to cool completely before slicing.

VARIATION

✦ Substitute green pepitas (squash seeds) or chopped walnuts for the sunflower seeds, or add extra nuts if you like the crunch.

PEAR STRUDEL
WITH BROWN SUGAR CREAM

❋ MAKES 2 STRUDEL, SERVING 6 ❋

DEBORAH REMEMBERS . . . *My aunt, my mother's youngest sister from Austria, came to live with us when I was born. She made great strudel, always starting with enormous sheets of dough. Many years later, when I had small children, she would come to visit us in San Diego and at the Ranch. When I'd tell the kids that Tanta was coming, their eyes would glow because she always came with two shoeboxes filled with different kinds of strudel. She probably baked for days before she got on the plane.*

Strudel was served almost every Friday at the Ranch for many years. It was economical: We always had some kind of local fruit, then just rolled out the dough, sprinkled on chopped nuts and fruit, and added lots of cinnamon and nutmeg. Foolproof! We never used phyllo dough then, but now it's an accepted shortcut.

5 TABLESPOONS PACKED BROWN SUGAR

3 TABLESPOONS SKINNED AND GROUND HAZELNUTS

1/4 TEASPOON GROUND CINNAMON

2 FIRM PEARS, PEELED AND CUT INTO 1/2-INCH DICE (ABOUT 2 1/2 CUPS; SEE NOTE)

1/3 CUP DRIED FRUIT, SUCH AS PRUNES, CRANBERRIES, CHERRIES, BLUEBERRIES, OR APRICOTS, AND CUT INTO SMALL PIECES

2 TEASPOONS FRESH LEMON JUICE

1 PACKAGE PHYLLO DOUGH, THAWED ACCORDING TO PACKAGE DIRECTIONS

1 1/2 TABLESPOONS BUTTER, MELTED

1/3 CUP THICK GREEK-STYLE YOGURT, *LABNA* (PAGE 60), OR SOUR CREAM

POWDERED SUGAR (OPTIONAL)

1. Preheat the oven to 350 degrees F.

2. In a small bowl, combine 1 tablespoon of the brown sugar, the nuts, and cinnamon.

3. In a medium bowl, combine the pears, dried fruit, lemon juice, and 2 tablespoons of the brown sugar.

4. Read package directions on phyllo dough. Lay out 1 sheet of phyllo, brush with melted butter, and sprinkle evenly with a small amount of the nut mixture. Top with a second sheet, squaring the edges. Brush with butter and sprinkle with additional nut mixture, leaving enough for the second strudel. Top with a third sheet. Place half of the fruit mixture across the short end, leaving a 1-inch margin on the three outer edges.

5. Fold the phyllo over the fruit once, tuck in the ends, and continue to roll all the way up. Set seam-side down on a baking sheet.

6. Repeat with 2 more phyllo sheets and the remaining nut and fruit mixtures. (Note: Any leftover phyllo may be rerolled, wrapped, and refrozen.)

7. Bake the strudel for 40 minutes or until the filling is soft and the phyllo is crisp and golden brown. Remove from the oven and cool for 5 minutes on a rack.

8. Make the Brown Sugar Cream by combining 2 tablespoons of the brown sugar and the yogurt, stirring until smooth. Refrigerate until ready to serve.

9. Cut the strudel into 1-inch-thick angled slices. Place 2 slices on each plate and dust with a little powdered sugar, if desired. Serve the sauce on the side.

NOTE: Don't use round Asian pears—they are watery when cooked.

THREE SISTERS MOLE

✦

THREE SISTERS BLACK MOLE

RICE, BEANS, AND CORN TORTILLAS

BUTTERNUT SQUASH FLAN

✦

The "Three Sisters"—corn, beans, and squash—were the essential foodstuffs of the ancient Americas. Mole is as venerable, and much more than a sauce—it is a meal in itself and is often eaten just with tortillas or bread, or in tamales.

Jesús learned to make authentic black mole from his mother, who grew up in a small town outside Mexico City. The unwritten recipe came to her from her mother, who learned it from her mother, and so on back through the generations. Jesús adapted the family recipe, focusing on the main ingredients to give the flavor, consistency, and color of a true black mole while slightly simplifying the process. Serve beans and corn tortillas with the mole for an authentic menu featuring all Three Sisters.

THREE SISTERS BLACK MOLE

❋ MAKES 8 CUPS ❋

For best flavor, use *mulato* chiles—they provide the essential subtle flavor and give the mole its black color. Serve the mole with any kind of cooked fish or tofu, as well as with beans and rice. It also tastes great on potatoes and other cooked vegetables. Always serve mole with lots of fresh, warm corn tortillas, though Jesús likes to eat it with bread. Serve with Frijoles Colorado de la Olla (page 152) and Mexican Red Rice (page 153).

4 LARGE DRY *GUAJILLO* CHILES, ABOUT 1 OUNCE

3 LARGE DRIED *MULATO* OR *PASILLA* CHILES, ABOUT 1 1/2 OUNCES

1/2 CUP RAW, SKINLESS PEANUTS

1/4 CUP WHOLE ALMONDS

ONE 3-INCH CINNAMON STICK

1 CORN TORTILLA, TORN INTO PIECES

1/4 CUP SESAME SEEDS

3 TABLESPOONS EXTRA-VIRGIN OLIVE OIL

3 CLOVES GARLIC, PEELED AND MINCED

1 LARGE WHITE ONION, PEELED AND CUT INTO 1/2-INCH DICE

3 OUNCES MEXICAN CHOCOLATE (IBARRA OR ABUELITA)

1/2 CUP TOMATO SAUCE OR 2 ROMA TOMATOES, CORED, SEEDED, AND CHOPPED

2 TEASPOONS SEA SALT

1/4 TEASPOON FRESH GROUND BLACK PEPPER

6 CUPS BASIC VEGETABLE STOCK (PAGE 176)

1. Preheat the oven to 350 degrees F.

2. Wearing gloves, remove the stems, seeds, and inner ribs from the chiles, and tear the chiles into large pieces.

3. Spread the peanuts, almonds, cinnamon stick, tortilla pieces, and sesame seeds on a large rimmed baking sheet. Toast in the oven for about 10 minutes, or until golden brown, being careful to not burn the sesame seeds.

4. In a large sauté pan, heat the olive oil over medium heat. Sauté the dried chiles, garlic, and onion, stirring constantly, for about 5 minutes, or until well blended and fragrant.

5. Add the toasted ingredients and cook, stirring constantly, for 5 minutes, being careful not to burn the chiles or nuts.

6. Break up the chocolate and add to the pan along with the tomato sauce, salt, and black pepper, and sauté for 3 minutes.

7. Add the stock and cook for 20 minutes at low heat.

8. Remove the cinnamon stick and discard. Put the mole in a blender jar and puree until very smooth. Refrigerate until ready to use, or for up to 3 days, or freeze for up to 6 months. Serve hot.

BUTTERNUT SQUASH FLAN

❉ SERVES 6 ❉

Traditional flan is creamy, rich, and heavy. This lightened version is based on naturally sweet butternut squash puree with a zing of orange in the syrup. Baked pureed yam may be substituted for the squash.

⅓ CUP PLUS ¼ CUP PACKED LIGHT BROWN SUGAR

3 TABLESPOONS FRESH ORANGE JUICE

3 CUPS MILK

4 EXTRA-LARGE EGGS

¾ CUP COOKED, PUREED BUTTERNUT SQUASH

1 TEASPOON GROUND CINNAMON

1 TEASPOON VANILLA EXTRACT

FINELY GRATED ZEST OF 1 ORANGE

SEASONAL FRUIT

1. Preheat the oven to 350 degrees F.

2. In a small saucepan, combine ⅓ cup of the brown sugar and the orange juice, and cook over low heat until the sugar is melted and bubbles form across the surface of the syrup, about 3 minutes.

3. Divide the syrup evenly among six 6-ounce ramekins.

4. In a medium saucepan, combine the milk and ¼ cup brown sugar. Heat over low to medium heat, stirring constantly, to dissolve the sugar. Set aside to cool.

5. In a bowl, whisk the eggs until frothy. Add the squash, cinnamon, vanilla, and orange zest. Stir in the cooled milk mixture. Strain the custard through a fine-mesh sieve to remove any traces of the squash fiber.

6. Divide the custard evenly among the ramekins, filling to within ¼ inch of the rim.

7. Place the ramekins in a rectangular baking pan with high sides and carefully pour 1 inch of boiling water into the pan. Cover with foil and bake on the middle rack of the oven for 30 minutes, or until the custards are no longer jiggly in the center and a toothpick inserted in the center comes out clean. Remove from the oven, take off the foil, and let the custards cool in the water bath. Once they are cool, remove from the pan, cover, and refrigerate for at least 3 hours.

8. To unmold, press gently around the edge of each flan to break the seal. Invert onto a dessert plate. If you prefer, the flan may be served right in the baking dish. Top with seasonal fruit.

EAT YOUR COLORS

The key to eating healthfully is to eat a wide variety of seasonal vegetables and fruits every day. But which are best for you? Consider using colors as your guide. Intense color usually indicates a high level of nutrients. For example, dark leafy greens like kale pack more nutritional wallop than pale-green delicate salad greens. Intensely orange squash is full of beta-carotenes. Brightly colored berries are full of antioxidants. Don't overlook pale foods like potatoes, though—these are a great source for minerals and vitamins, and for valuable carbohydrates.

TECATE SUNSHINE

✦

MARKET VEGETABLE SOUP

SPICY JICAMA PEPPER SLAW WITH MINT-JALAPEÑO DRESSING

RANCH CHILES RELLENOS WITH ANCHO CHILE SALSA

COCONUT ICE
WITH CHOCOLATE DRIZZLE AND PEANUTS

✦

Rancho La Puerta lies near the Baja town of Tecate, a place high in the mountains where the air is clear as glass, the sky a distinctive blue, and the sun shines nearly every day. But the real sunshine comes from the wide smiles of the friendly and hospitable Tecateños, who are proud of their lovely mountain pueblo. This menu is a tribute to the fresh Mexican flavors that you can find any day in Tecate.

MARKET VEGETABLE SOUP

❋ MAKES 4 QUARTS ❋

Soup is an easy, delicious way to get your vegetables. A visit to the market allows you to stock up on what's freshest that week. Be sure to choose lots of colors for your soup—flavor comes from variety. Make a big pot of soup and maybe a loaf of bread to go with it. The soup will keep, refrigerated, for a couple of days. Freeze extra soup in plastic freezer bags for a quick, healthy meal.

1 1/2 TEASPOONS OLIVE OIL

1 LARGE LEEK, WHITE PART ONLY, WASHED AND CUT INTO 1-INCH PIECES

1 SMALL CARROT, PEELED AND CUT INTO 1/2-INCH DICE

1/2 MEDIUM ONION, CUT INTO 1/4-INCH DICE

1/2 STALK CELERY, CUT INTO 1/4-INCH DICE

3 CLOVES GARLIC, PEELED AND MINCED

1 TABLESPOON GROUND CALIFORNIA CHILES OR GROUND CURRY

7 CUPS BASIC VEGETABLE STOCK (PAGE 176)

4 ROMA TOMATOES, CORED

4 CUPS ASSORTED COLORFUL SEASONAL VEGETABLES (SUCH AS CAULIFLOWER, BROCCOLI, CARROTS, SWEET POTATOES, SQUASH, RED OR GREEN BELL PEPPERS, TURNIPS, KOHLRABI, PARSNIPS, CELERY ROOT, MUSHROOMS, CORN, OR PEAS), CUT INTO 1/2-INCH DICE

1 BAY LEAF

2 TEASPOONS SEA SALT, OR MORE TO TASTE

1/2 TEASPOON FRESH GROUND BLACK PEPPER

1 SMALL BUNCH DARK LEAFY GREENS, SUCH AS SPINACH OR KALE, STEMMED AND ROUGHLY CHOPPED

1/2 CUP FRESH FLAT-LEAF PARSLEY LEAVES, ROUGHLY CHOPPED

2 TABLESPOONS CHOPPED FRESH BASIL

1. In a 6-quart stockpot, heat the oil over medium heat. Cook the leek, carrot, onion, celery, and garlic, stirring often, until the vegetables start to soften, about 5 minutes.

2. Add the ground chiles and cook for 1 minute to develop the flavor. Add 6 cups of the stock and bring to a simmer.

3. In a blender, puree 2 of the tomatoes with the remaining 1 cup stock, and add to the soup. Seed and cut the other 2 tomatoes into 1/2-inch dice and add to the soup.

4. When the soup begins to simmer, add the assorted vegetables, bay leaf, salt, and pepper.

5. Simmer the soup until the vegetables are tender, about 45 minutes. Stir in the chopped greens, parsley, and basil, and cook 5 minutes more. Taste for seasoning, and add salt, if needed.

VARIATIONS
At the end...

✦ Add a handful of cooked brown rice, barley, or bulgur wheat (see page 166).

✦ Add 1 cup of precooked beans, such as garbanzos, black beans, kidney beans, lima beans, or white beans (see page 177).

✦ Add roasted corn.

✦ Puree the entire soup.

SPICY JICAMA PEPPER SLAW
WITH MINT-JALAPEÑO DRESSING

❋ SERVES 6 ❋

Beautiful firm cabbages, glowing peppers, fat orange carrots, and row upon row of Florence fennel. What do you do with all this bounty? Jesús makes salads like this hearty slaw, colorful and delicious. Feel free to mix and match ingredients, depending on what you find at your farmers' market.

1 CUP CUBED JICAMA

1 RED BELL PEPPER, CUT INTO ½-INCH DICE OR JULIENNE

1 STALK CELERY, THINLY SLICED

1 BULB FENNEL, TRIMMED AND THINLY SLICED

2 CUPS FINELY SHREDDED GREEN AND RED CABBAGE

2 CUPS SHREDDED PEELED CARROTS

MINT-JALAPEÑO DRESSING (RECIPE FOLLOWS)

4 CUPS BABY SPINACH OR MIXED GREENS

In a large bowl, combine the first 6 ingredients with the dressing, enough to moisten, and marinate for several hours. Just before serving, toss the slaw with the spinach and some additional dressing, if desired.

VARIATION

✦ During corn season, add 1 cup cooked corn to the salad before chilling.

MINT-JALAPEÑO DRESSING

❋ MAKES 2 CUPS ❋

This is a dynamite dressing, one you will make again and again. Jesús frequently uses mint in surprising ways, usually to balance heat and add freshness—a secret ingredient that lifts flavors up without giving itself away. Either spearmint or peppermint (*yerba buena*) does the trick. If you fear the jalapeño, substitute a piece of mild green or red bell pepper.

3 LARGE SHALLOTS, PEELED AND ROUGHLY CHOPPED

1 CUP FRESH MINT LEAVES, OR A COMBINATION OF MINT AND BASIL

1 JALAPEÑO, SEEDS AND RIBS REMOVED, ROUGHLY CHOPPED

1 CUP WATER

½ CUP RED WINE VINEGAR

¼ CUP AGAVE SYRUP OR HONEY

1 TEASPOON SEA SALT, OR TO TASTE

⅛ TEASPOON FRESH GROUND BLACK PEPPER

In a blender, combine all of the ingredients, pulsing until smooth.

RANCH CHILES RELLENOS
WITH ANCHO CHILE SALSA

❋ SERVES 6 ❋

DEBORAH REMEMBERS . . . *Chiles Rellenos have been a Ranch standard from day one. I've never had anyone say, "I don't like them," and lots of guests absolutely rave about them. They're one of my most favorite dinners or lunches, and I especially like them with tangy Jack cheese.*

Dark-green, shiny poblano chiles are the traditional choice for chiles rellenos. They have great flavor, but may be too spicy for some tastes. Anaheim chiles or colorful red chiles are reliably mild substitutes. You can stuff chiles with almost anything: cheese, shrimp, smoked fish, tuna and sour cream, grilled vegetables, crabmeat. You get the idea. For a larger crowd, the recipe can be doubled. For an appetizer or cocktail nibble, stuff small colorful peppers. Serve the rellenos with beans and rice—Black Beans with Epazote (page 92), Frijoles Colorado de la Olla (page 152), refried beans, or Mexican Red Rice (page 153).

6 POBLANO OR ANAHEIM CHILES

4 OUNCES MONTEREY JACK CHEESE, CUT INTO 6 LONG STRIPS

1/4 TEASPOON DRIED MEXICAN OREGANO

1/4 CUP ALL-PURPOSE FLOUR

1/4 TEASPOON SEA SALT

1 TABLESPOON VEGETABLE OIL

1 EXTRA-LARGE EGG WHITE, BEATEN UNTIL LIGHT AND FROTHY

ANCHO CHILE SALSA (PAGE 39)

1. Preheat the oven to 400 degrees F.

2. Char the chiles on all sides directly over a gas flame until the skin blackens and blisters, or broil directly under a hot broiler until the skin begins to pull away from the pepper. Wrap in paper towels until cool.

3. Handle the peppers carefully so they do not tear. Use the paper towel to rub off the blistered skin. Leave the stems on. Make a 2-inch slit lengthwise in each chile and remove the seeds. Tuck a piece of cheese into each chile and fold the chile over to completely enclose the cheese, so it doesn't ooze out when it melts.

4. Over a small bowl, rub the oregano between your palms to bring out the flavor. Add the flour and salt and stir to combine mixture. Spread the flour on a plate.

5. In a 10-inch sauté pan, heat the oil over medium heat. Dip each chile into the flour to coat on all sides, and brush off any excess, then dip into the egg white. Carefully set into the hot pan and cook until the cheese is melted and the chiles are golden brown on both sides. Serve with warm salsa.

VARIATION

✦ Make a summer corn filling by sautéing 1/4 cup chopped onion and 1 clove minced garlic in 1/2 teaspoon olive oil, until the onion is translucent. Add 1/2 cup cooked corn and 1/4 cup finely chopped red bell pepper or Roma tomato. Cook until just tender. Cool and add to 1/2 cup ricotta cheese along with 1/4 cup grated Jack cheese and 1 tablespoon chopped cilantro.

COCONUT ICE WITH CHOCOLATE DRIZZLE AND PEANUTS

❋ MAKES 4 CUPS ❋

This sophisticated sorbet is rich and smooth with coconut milk, made sumptuous with a drizzle of dark chocolate and a sprinkling of crunchy nuts. Make the portions small—a little goes a long way.

1 ½ CUPS MILK

1 CAN (13.5 OUNCES) COCONUT MILK

6 TABLESPOONS BROWN SUGAR

1 TABLESPOON VANILLA BEAN PASTE OR PURE VANILLA EXTRACT

2 TABLESPOONS FRESH LIME JUICE

2 OUNCES SEMISWEET CHOCOLATE, BROKEN INTO SMALL PIECES

2 TABLESPOONS CHOPPED TOASTED PEANUTS

1. In a 2-quart saucepan, combine 1 ¼ cups of the milk, coconut milk, brown sugar, vanilla, and lime juice. Stir over low heat until the sugar is dissolved. Pour into a bowl, cover, and chill thoroughly, about 2 hours.

2. Freeze in an ice cream maker according to manufacturer's directions. Alternatively, pour into a shallow pan and freeze, stirring once every hour for several hours. When it is solid, break into small cubes, soften at room temperature for 15 minutes, and grind until smooth in a food processor. It will stay creamy when refrozen. (This recipe may be made up to this point up to 48 hours before serving.)

3. Make the Chocolate Drizzle by heating the remaining ¼ cup of milk in a small saucepan over low heat. Remove from the heat, add the chocolate, and stir until smooth. Keep warm until ready to serve.

4. Soften the ice cream at room temperature for about 20 minutes. Scoop ½-cup servings into small bowls. Drizzle each serving with 1 tablespoon of the sauce and sprinkle with 1 teaspoon peanuts.

VARIATIONS

✦ Serve a scoop of sorbet on top of a slice of warm grilled pineapple.

✦ Substitute crushed toasted macadamia nuts, cashews, or other nuts for the peanuts.

✦ Vegans may substitute soy, rice, or almond milk for the dairy.

"EMBRACE THE LIMITATIONS OF THE SEASON."
FERGUS HENDERSON

All of Tres Estrellas is quiet during this time of waiting between the fall harvest and the winter rains. Flocks of birds rise and fall against the mountainside and grey-green chaparral, feeding on clusters of tiny red mesquite berries and gleaning seeds among rows of dark green arugula. Jewel-filled pomegranates hang among tattered leaves like Chinese lanterns, split open by their own tart juice. Forgotten pears dangle high on nearly bare trees. ✦ The nights are cold, still, and clear as glass. A full moon shines on boulders shattered by eons of heat and cold. Stars sparkle pale pink and gold in the hollow night sky; they seem close enough to touch, hung three-dimensionally in bottomless space. Sometimes, in the morning, there is frost on the brick pathways. ✦ The garden is forever being born, then dying—from spring's energetic burst, through summer's abundant foliage, into a fall exhausted from bearing, to winter where the silent work of regeneration and renewal takes

WINTER
Rebirth

place. ✦ So much of what goes on in the garden is invisible and unknowable. Plants grow where they fall, or are put. They set roots into the stony, tired ground in imperfect weather, yet somehow flourish. When they wither away, not exactly dying, they go back into the earth to nourish a precarious future. Plants bridge mineral and animal worlds, bringing life and water out of the earth, opening to and interacting with sun and weather. Trample them, burn them, yank them out, and in no time, they're back. Pave them over with cold concrete and, through a crack, will pop a strand of green—a reminder that the green up-swelling under our feet is unstoppable. The need for a seed to live, to force its roots down and reach for the sky, is one of the great forces in nature. This connection to a bigger world is something we have, too, and forget until we hear the whispers from beneath our feet.

Winter Sun

✦

ENDIVE AND GRAPE SALAD

MUSHROOM QUICHE WITH GOAT CHEESE

CHOCOLATE BANANA BREAD

✦

*Enjoy a few classics: a salad of mildly bitter winter lettuces and sweet grapes,
mushroom quiche with creamy goat cheese, and something warm and
sweet for dessert. Jesús' terrifically indulgent Chocolate Banana Bread
is gooey enough for chocoholics, but it is made with healthy ingredients.
The quiche and bread can share oven time.*

ENDIVE AND GRAPE SALAD

❀ SERVES 6 ❀

In 1940, the Ranch was little more than a small adobe house and rows of gnarled old grape vines. Hungry guests trolling for snacks would sometimes strip the vines bare of grapes. Grapes still find their way to the kitchen, where they are used on fruit plates, in salads, or in *agua fresca* (page 34). Jesús likes the look of tiny champagne grapes on this salad. You could substitute any dried fruit for the blueberries and raisins.

3 CUPS BABY SPINACH OR OTHER MILD-FLAVORED GREENS

4 BELGIAN ENDIVE OR RED ENDIVE, CUT INTO 1-INCH PIECES

1/3 CUP BASIL BALSAMIC DRESSING (PAGE 79)

2 CUPS GRAPES

1/2 CUP CRUMBLED BLUE CHEESE, SUCH AS GORGONZOLA, STILTON, OR DOMESTIC BLUE CHEESE

1/2 CUP TOASTED PECANS

2 TABLESPOONS DRIED BLUEBERRIES

2 TABLESPOONS GOLDEN RAISINS

Just before serving, toss the spinach and endive with the dressing. Divide among 6 plates and top with some grapes, cheese, pecans, blueberries, and raisins.

DEBORAH'S COOKING TIPS FOR MODIFYING RECIPES

✦ Buy fresh, buy organic, buy local, and buy what's in season (see page 37).

✦ Find ways to add fresh vegetables to every bite you eat. Add chopped vegetables to salads, rice, sauces, and pastas sauces. Make fresh soups. There's a thousand ways to do this—get cooking!

✦ Swap refined flours and grains for whole grains and whole wheat. Whole *anything* is better than refined.

✦ Reduce your automatic oil use. You need less oil than you think to sauté or to make a dressing. Use olive oil exclusively, and put some in a spray bottle, so you can use a squirt or two instead of pouring it on.

✦ Combine legumes and whole grains for extra nutrition; these are often hearty enough to make a meal if accompanied by vegetables.

✦ Add nuts to almost anything to add flavor and crunch.

✦ Reduce the fat and salt in your recipe by using herbs to enhance the flavor.

MUSHROOM QUICHE WITH GOAT CHEESE

❋ SERVES 6 ❋

DEBORAH REMEMBERS . . . *In the early days, when we had our own goats, we made cheese and used it in every way. One of our favorite recipes was a mushroom quiche. We didn't have exotic mushrooms, of course, but we had plenty of oregano and fresh basil to add that perfect herbal note that our guests still love. The flavors are made for each other.*

Quiche is easy to make and good for you, too. This is a good basic quiche recipe that may be varied by using any vegetables, adding different herbs to the crust or leaving them out, changing the cheese, and so on, though this mushroom-dill filling is so savory and good, you may never change it. Jesús likes to use mild-flavored mushrooms, such as oyster, button, and portobello.

The quiche, crust and all, may be prepared in the time it takes for the oven to heat up. Or you may prepare everything a day or two before, keeping the filling and crust separate, and bake it just before serving. Double the recipe to make 2 pie crusts and freeze one for later. Little miniature quiches, baked in muffin tins or tartlet shells, are a terrific party food.

QUICHE CRUST

⅓ CUP UNSALTED BUTTER, CHILLED

1½ CUPS UNBLEACHED ALL-PURPOSE FLOUR

1 TEASPOON CHOPPED FRESH THYME

⅛ TEASPOON SALT

¼ TEASPOON FRESH GROUND BLACK PEPPER

1½ TABLESPOONS ICE WATER

1 TEASPOON WHITE VINEGAR

MUSHROOM FILLING

1 TEASPOON EXTRA-VIRGIN OLIVE OIL

¼ RED ONION, PEELED AND DICED (ABOUT ½ CUP)

1 LARGE CLOVE GARLIC, PEELED AND MINCED

4 OUNCES MIXED EXOTIC MUSHROOMS (OYSTER, CREMINI, PORTOBELLO, OR WHITE BUTTON MUSHROOMS), STEMMED AND CUT INTO ½-INCH PIECES (ABOUT 2 CUPS)

8 EGG WHITES

4 WHOLE EGGS

6 FRESH BASIL LEAVES, CHOPPED (ABOUT 2 TABLESPOONS)

2 TEASPOONS CHOPPED FRESH OREGANO LEAVES

⅛ TEASPOON FRESH GRATED NUTMEG

¼ TEASPOON WHITE PEPPER

½ TEASPOON SEA SALT

4 OUNCES GOAT CHEESE, IMPORTED SWISS CHEESE, OR SMOKED GOUDA, GRATED

1. Preheat the oven to 350 degrees F.

2. To make the crust, cut the butter into small pieces and place in the bowl a food processor with the flour, thyme, salt, and ⅛ teaspoon of the pepper. Pulse several times to combine. Pieces of butter should still be visible. Mix the water and vinegar and slowly add to the flour mixture, pulsing to combine as you do so, until the mixture sticks together when pinched.

3. Turn the dough out onto a piece of plastic wrap and form it into a ball. Cover with another piece of plastic and, using a rolling pin, flatten the dough into a circle about 4 inches across. Refrigerate the dough for 15 minutes while you make the filling.

4. In a sauté pan, heat the oil over medium heat and sauté the onion and garlic for 2 minutes, stirring often. Add the mushrooms and continue to cook 5 minutes, or until the mushrooms are soft and there is no liquid in the pan. Set aside to cool.

5. After the dough has rested, roll it out between the sheets of plastic to fit a 9-inch pie tin. Peel the plastic off the top and lay the crust over the rolling pin to transport it, turning it upside down into a pie tin and peeling off the other sheet of plastic. Gently press the crust into the pie tin and trim the edges. If you like, give the edges a decorative fluting. (The crust may be made ahead to this point and refrigerated for 1 day or frozen for up to 1 month.)

6. Thoroughly combine the egg whites and whole eggs. Add the oregano, basil, nutmeg, white pepper, sea salt, and black pepper.

7. Place the pie tin on a baking sheet, scatter the cheeses and sautéed mushrooms in the crust, and pour the egg mixture over the filling.

8. Bake for 35 to 40 minutes, or until the quiche is slightly puffed, springy to the touch, and a toothpick or skewer inserted in the center comes out clean.

VARIATIONS

✦ Make the filling with 8 whole eggs, instead of the whites and whole eggs combination.

✦ Make the crust with ¾ cup whole-wheat flour and ¾ cup unbleached all-purpose flour.

CHOCOLATE BANANA BREAD

❈ MAKES 1 LOAF ❈

This bread is chocolate heaven, really—a rich, dark, dense loaf, made with ripe bananas and pureed prunes, that tastes far more sinful than it really is. Serve warm, sliced thin, with fresh fruit, or freeze for up to 1 month.

2 CUPS WATER

12 OUNCES PITTED PRUNES

2 MEDIUM RIPE BANANAS

2 LARGE EGGS

1 CUP UNBLEACHED ALL-PURPOSE OR WHOLE-WHEAT FLOUR

1/2 CUP COCOA POWDER

1 TABLESPOON GROUND CINNAMON

2 TEASPOONS BAKING POWDER

1 1/2 TEASPOONS BAKING SODA

1 CUP CHOPPED WALNUTS

1/2 CUP BANANA CHIPS, BROKEN INTO SMALL PIECES

1 CUP SEMISWEET CHOCOLATE CHIPS

1. Preheat the oven to 350 degrees F. Lightly butter an 8-cup loaf pan, and line the bottom with a piece of parchment paper.

2. In a small saucepan, combine the water and prunes and bring to a simmer. Simmer slowly until the prunes are very soft, about 30 minutes. Drain any excess liquid.

3. Puree the prunes, bananas, and eggs in a blender until smooth.

4. Sift together the flour, cocoa, cinnamon, baking powder, and baking soda into a large bowl. Stir in the banana mixture and combine thoroughly. Gently stir in the walnuts, banana chips, and chocolate chips. Pour the batter into the prepared pan and bake for 50 to 60 minutes, or until a sharp knife inserted in the center comes out clean (or with only a bit of melted chocolate chip on it).

5. Turn the loaf out onto a rack to cool, and remove the parchment from the bottom. Cut into thin slices to serve.

REDUCING FATS IN BAKING

If you have a favorite quick bread or muffin recipe that contains shortening or oil, try substituting one of these healthy alternatives for some or all of the fat in the recipe. They can also thicken sauces and dressings.

✦ Thick applesauce

✦ Pureed bananas or peaches

✦ Prunes, apricots, or other dried fruit that has been soaked in a small amount of hot water, drained, and pureed smooth in a blender

SOLSTICE CELEBRATION

✦

SQUASH-APPLE SOUP WITH THAI RED CURRY

GLAZED ROASTED SALMON EN CROÛTE

ROOT VEGETABLES ROASTED WITH HONEY, BALSAMIC, AND SPICES

CARROT-PINEAPPLE CAKE WITH APRICOT CREAM FROSTING

✦

Even in the longest winter, the solstice always comes—that magic day when the sun turns back to us and the days start to become longer, heading inexorably to summer. Ancient cultures marked this important day with celebration, and more than a little relief. This menu is full of the nourishing, warm tastes of the season, but looks a bit wistfully toward spring.

SQUASH-APPLE SOUP
WITH THAI RED CURRY

✸ SERVES 6 ✸

The colorful kings of the winter garden, squash of all types are packed with beta-carotene and other vital nutrients. Plus, they taste divinely buttery and sweet. Salvador has grown many varieties of squash at Tres Estrellas over the years, but has settled on acorn and butternut (with the occasional pumpkin) as the most practical for kitchen use.

Thai curry paste gives a tiny zing of spice to balance the sweetness of the soup. For a very special occasion you could serve the soup in hollowed out miniature pumpkins or small squash.

2 TEASPOONS OLIVE OIL

1 SMALL BUTTERNUT SQUASH, PEELED, SEEDED, AND CUBED (ABOUT 4 CUPS)

1 APPLE, CORED, PEELED, AND DICED

2 LEEKS, WHITE PART ONLY, WASHED AND SLICED

1 SMALL CARROT, PEELED AND SLICED

1/2 STALK CELERY, FINELY CHOPPED

1 TABLESPOON CHOPPED FRESH BASIL

2 TEASPOONS THAI RED CURRY PASTE (SEE NOTE)

4 CUPS BASIC VEGETABLE STOCK (PAGE 176)

2 CUPS WATER

1 TABLESPOON BROWN SUGAR

2 TEASPOONS SEA SALT, OR MORE TO TASTE

THINLY SLICED CHIVES

THIN STRIPS OF ORANGE ZEST (OPTIONAL)

1. In a 4-quart saucepan, heat the olive oil over medium heat. Add the squash, apple, leeks, carrot, celery, and basil and cook, stirring often, until the vegetables are softened; do not brown. Add the curry paste and cook, stirring constantly, for 1 minute. Add the stock, water, brown sugar, and salt. Reduce the heat to medium-low and simmer for 45 minutes, or until the vegetables are very soft.

2. Cool for 30 minutes, then, in a blender or in the bowl of a food processor, puree until absolutely smooth.

3. Reheat and taste for seasoning, adding salt if needed. Serve very hot, with a sprinkling of chives and the orange and zest, if desired.

NOTE: Thai red curry paste tastes nothing like Indian curry. Sold in small jars, the paste is pungent and quite spicy, and it will last months in the refrigerator.

VARIATION

✦ To prepare squash bowls, choose small acorn squash or pumpkins no more than 6 inches in diameter. Scrub the squash in cold water. Cut off the top quarter of the squash—saving it to use as a lid—and a small slice from the bottom, so the squash sits flat without wobbling. (With the harder varieties, you may need to use a saw.) Scoop out the insides to create a cavity large enough to hold 8 ounces of soup. Brush inside and out with oil and bake for 15 minutes at 400 degrees F, until shiny and lightly browned but still very firm. Use within 24 hours.

GLAZED ROASTED SALMON EN CROÛTE

❋ SERVES 6 TO 8 ❋

This beautiful, phyllo-wrapped Wellington looks impressive, but it is quick and remarkably easy to make. Sliced, it reveals layers of pink salmon, sautéed spinach, and rice, speckled with sweet peppers. Jesús prefers the taste and color of wild trolled salmon, which also contains more healthy omega-3 fats.

For a larger group, double the recipe and make two this size—it's easier to handle than one large one. Use a serrated knife to cut 1-inch slices, or serve it buffet style.

¼ CUP PLUS 1 TEASPOON OLIVE OIL, PLUS MORE TO SPRAY THE PHYLLO

⅓ CUP DICED RED BELL PEPPER

2 CLOVES GARLIC, PEELED AND MINCED

¼ CUP FINELY DICED WHITE ONION

6 OUNCES FRESH SPINACH, STEMMED AND ROUGHLY CHOPPED

1½ CUPS COOKED BROWN RICE, WILD RICE, OR WHOLE-WHEAT COUSCOUS (SEE PAGE 166)

2 GREEN ONIONS, THINLY SLICED

2 TABLESPOONS CHOPPED FRESH DILL

2 TABLESPOONS FRESH LEMON JUICE

1 TEASPOON SALT

1 PACKAGE PHYLLO DOUGH, THAWED ACCORDING TO PACKAGE DIRECTIONS

2-POUND SALMON FILET, SKINLESS (PREFERABLY A CENTER PIECE)

SEA SALT AND FRESH GROUND BLACK PEPPER

2 TABLESPOONS AGAVE SYRUP

LEMON ZEST AIOLI (PAGE 113)

LEMON WEDGES

1 TABLESPOON DRAINED CAPERS

1. Preheat the oven to 375 degrees F.

2. In a large sauté pan, heat 1 teaspoon of the oil. Cook the bell pepper, garlic, and white onion until slightly softened. Add the spinach and cook, stirring, until the spinach is wilted.

3. Stir in the rice, green onions, dill, lemon juice, and salt. Taste for seasoning—it should be strongly seasoned. Set aside to cool.

4. Unfold the phyllo sheets. Lay 1 sheet out on a baking sheet or cutting board and spray the dough lightly with oil. Next, lay 2 sheets over the first one, slightly overlapping the sheets to make a 14 × 18-inch rectangle. Brush the dough with olive oil. Repeat 4 more times. (To prevent drying, always keep the phyllo dough covered with a dry kitchen towel when not in use.)

5. Run your fingers over the salmon and remove any small bones you feel. Trim away any dark flesh or fat along the thin (belly) edge. Season well on both sides with salt and pepper.

6. Drizzle the syrup over the salmon, sprinkle lightly with salt, and place the salmon, skin-side (gray marks) up, in the center of the phyllo sheets. Spoon the spinach mixture on top of the salmon and pat into an even layer.

7. Fold the short sides of the phyllo over the salmon, then firmly fold the other two sides in to make a neat, firm package. Flip the package over onto a lightly oiled baking sheet, and bake for 30 minutes until crisp and golden-brown and the internal temperature measures 150 degrees F.

8. Let the salmon rest for at least 15 minutes. Then, using a sharp, serrated knife, slice the salmon into 1-inch slices and serve with the aioli, lemon wedges, and a few capers on the side.

VARIATIONS

✦ Sprinkle chopped fresh herbs, such as dill or tarragon, between the layers of phyllo.

✦ Add ¼ cup chopped sun-dried tomatoes to the rice mixture.

ROOT VEGETABLES ROASTED WITH HONEY, BALSAMIC, AND SPICES

❄ SERVES 6 ❄

The winter root cellar has plenty of unusual vegetables deserving of your attention. Most are usually served boiled or mashed, but here slow oven-roasting gives each vegetable a distinctive character that is only enhanced by a drizzle of honey and a sprinkling of Jesús' spice rub. Jesús uses this aromatic blend of spices on grilled vegetables and tofu. Keep any extra spice mix in a tightly sealed jar.

1 TABLESPOON WHOLE FENNEL SEED

1 TEASPOON CRUSHED RED PEPPER

1 TEASPOON WHOLE DRIED THYME

1/2 TEASPOON SEA SALT

1/2 TEASPOON FRESH GROUND BLACK PEPPER

1/2 TEASPOON GROUND ALLSPICE

2 SMALL PARSNIPS

1 LARGE CARROT

1 CHAYOTE

1/2 WHITE TURNIP

1/2 RUTABAGA

2 CUPS ADDITIONAL VEGETABLES, SUCH AS SHALLOTS, SWEET POTATOES OR YAMS, PURPLE POTATOES, OR WINTER SQUASH

2 TEASPOONS OLIVE OIL

2 TEASPOONS BALSAMIC VINEGAR

1 TEASPOON HONEY

1. Preheat the oven to 400 degrees F.

2. Heat a small frying pan over medium heat. Add the fennel seed and toast, shaking constantly, until the seeds are fragrant, about 1 minute. Pour onto a plate to cool. Stir in the remaining spices.

3. Peel the vegetables and cut into 1½-inch chunks. In a large bowl, toss the vegetables with 1 tablespoon of the spice mixture and oil.

4. Spread the seasoned vegetables on a baking sheet in a single layer—do not crowd them together or they won't roast properly.

5. Roast for 45 minutes, or until the vegetables are well-browned and soft. Loosen the vegetables from the pan with a thin spatula and drizzle with the vinegar and honey.

VARIATIONS

✦ Substitute chopped rosemary for the spice rub.

✦ Add 1 tablespoon chopped garlic to the balsamic and honey before drizzling.

TOASTING AND GRINDING SPICES

For vibrant flavor, whole spices should be toasted and ground fresh as you need them. Place spices in a dry sauté pan over medium heat and toast, shaking gently, until fragrant. Cool to room temperature, then grind to a fine powder in a spice grinder or a coffee grinder used exclusively for spices, or with a mortar and pestle. Every spice benefits from this treatment, including black peppercorns.

CARROT-PINEAPPLE CAKE
WITH APRICOT CREAM FROSTING

❋ MAKES ONE 8-INCH CAKE ❋

Most carrot cakes deliver healthy ingredients with loads of fat. In this very simple, moist cake, applesauce is substituted for the usual oil, and crushed pineapple adds moistness and flavor. The cake is delicious even without the creamy frosting—try serving it lightly dusted with powdered sugar, alongside a citrus salad or fresh pineapple.

2 EGGS

ZEST OF 1 ORANGE

3/4 CUP PACKED BROWN SUGAR

1/2 CUP APPLESAUCE

1 TEASPOON PURE VANILLA EXTRACT

1 CUP WHOLE-WHEAT FLOUR

1 CUP ALL-PURPOSE FLOUR

2 TEASPOONS BAKING POWDER

1 TEASPOON BAKING SODA

2 CUPS GRATED CARROTS

1 1/4 CUPS DRAINED CRUSHED PINEAPPLE IN JUICE

1/2 CUP SHREDDED COCONUT, SWEETENED OR UNSWEETENED

APRICOT CREAM FROSTING

6 DRIED APRICOTS, CUT INTO 1/4-INCH DICE

4 OUNCES NEUFCHÂTEL OR LOW-FAT CREAM CHEESE

1/2 CUP POWDERED SUGAR, SIFTED

1/4 TEASPOON PURE VANILLA EXTRACT

1. Preheat the oven to 350 degrees F. Lightly brush an 8-inch cake pan with oil.

2. Beat the eggs with the orange zest and sugar until thick. Stir in the applesauce and the vanilla.

3. Sift the flours, baking powder, and baking soda into a large bowl. Stir the egg mixture into the flour mixture, then fold in the carrots, pineapple, and coconut.

4. Spoon the batter into the prepared cake pan and bake for 35 to 40 minutes, or until a skewer inserted in the center of the cake comes out clean.

5. Cool the cake in the pan for 10 minutes, then turn out onto a rack and cool completely.

6. To make the frosting, soak the apricots in hot water until they are very soft. Drain thoroughly.

7. With a hand mixer, whip the Neufchâtel until smooth and fluffy. Beat in the powdered sugar and the 1/4 teaspoon of vanilla. Fold in the apricots. Spread the frosting evenly over the top of the cooled cake, and cut into thin wedges to serve.

VARIATIONS

✦ Add 1/2 cup golden raisins, soaked in hot water and drained, to the batter.

✦ Sprinkle the chopped apricots over the frosted cake instead of folding them into the frosting.

✦ Add 1/3 cup chopped toasted pecans to the batter or sprinkle over the frosted cake.

✦ Bake in a loaf pan (at 350 degrees for 50 minutes) or lined muffin cups (at 350 degrees for 25 minutes).

QUICK
WEEKDAY DINNER

✦

CAESAR SALAD PROVENÇALE

STIR-FRIED SCALLOPS
WITH SUN-DRIED TOMATOES AND BABY BOK CHOY

BROILED ORANGES WITH HONEY YOGURT AND PISTACHIOS

✦

*Stir-frying is the quickest way to cook anything, and the rest of this menu
is equally fast and simple. Start with the Ranch's version of the classic
Caesar salad and finish with a treat—juicy broiled oranges served
with thick, creamy, honey-sweetened yogurt.*

CAESAR SALAD PROVENÇALE

※ SERVES 6 ※

Fall and winter are romaine season at Tres Estrellas, with rows of the tall, tightly furled heads ready to be turned into this favorite Ranch salad. Baby lettuces may dominate the salad world, but there is no substitute for the crispness of a mature lettuce like romaine when it's tossed with a good flavorful dressing.

Caesar salad is believed to have originated in the 1920s down the road from the Ranch in Tijuana at the Hotel Caesar. The original version is made with raw egg yolks and plenty of oil and garlic. The Ranch makes a significantly lightened version of the dressing and gives the salad a Mediterranean spin with the addition of Greek olives and tomatoes. The traditional Caesar is a knife and fork salad, made only with whole leaves from the tender romaine hearts. If you prefer, chop the hearts instead of serving them whole.

2 TABLESPOONS ANCHOVY PASTE, OR 2 ANCHOVY FILETS, MINCED

CREAMY ASIAGO DRESSING (PAGE 112)

3 MEDIUM HEADS ROMAINE LETTUCE

1 MEDIUM CUCUMBER, PEELED, SEEDED, AND SLICED

3 MEDIUM ROMA TOMATOES, CORED, HALVED, AND SLICED

6 ANCHOVY FILETS (OPTIONAL)

¼ CUP KALAMATA OLIVES, PITTED AND CUT IN HALF

6 THIN SLICES RED ONION

2 TABLESPOONS CAPERS

¼ CUP GRATED ASIAGO CHEESE

1. Add the anchovy to the dressing and taste (you may want to add more lemon).

2. Remove and discard the dark green outer leaves of the lettuce until you reach the crisp hearts. The outer leaves are bitter and flabby—only the hearts of the romaine should be eaten. Separate the hearts, wash, and dry. Leave whole and chill until ready to serve.

3. In a large bowl, toss the romaine hearts with just enough dressing to lightly coat each leaf. Divide among 6 chilled plates so the leaves are all pointing in the same direction. Top each salad with the cucumbers and tomatoes, and a single anchovy filet, if desired. Garnish with olives, red onion, and capers, and sprinkle the cheese over the salads. Serve with extra dressing on the side.

STIR-FRIED SCALLOPS WITH SUN-DRIED TOMATOES AND BABY BOK CHOY

❄ SERVES 6 ❄

DEBORAH REMEMBERS . . . *We have the most marvelous seafood in Baja California, and most of it comes to us via the fishing ports of Ensenada on the Pacific side or San Felipe on the Gulf side. If you live on the East Coast and love shellfish, I know you already have a favorite source for scallops. They're precious wherever you find them, and you might hesitate to prepare them this way, preferring instead to pan-fry them and present them three or four on a plate like steep-sided round islands. But give stir-frying a try. It's healthier, and the scallops pair with the bok choy in a way that is very special.*

The essential part of this recipe is the stir-fry technique. Once you know the basic steps, the variations are almost infinite. No wok is required; you can use a large sauté pan. (Refer to page 186 for more about the stir-fry technique.) Make sure everything is ready to cook before you turn on the flame, because the cooking goes quickly and you do not want to overcook the scallops or they will be dry and chewy.

Choy are members of a large Asian family of greens that Salvador grows in heroic quantities for use at the Ranch. At any size, choy are tender and quick-cooking and have a mild flavor. Though the recipe calls for baby bok choy, which are typically 4 to 6 inches long and cook in a flash, you may substitute sliced mature choy. Visit an Asian supermarket and check out the produce section for interesting greens and herbs to experiment with. Anything that looks like choy probably is, and it may be substituted for the greens mentioned here.

---

2 TABLESPOONS OLIVE OIL

1 MEDIUM WHITE ONION, PEELED, HALVED, AND SLICED INTO 1/4-INCH PIECES

3 CLOVES GARLIC, PEELED AND MINCED

12 LARGE SCALLOPS, QUARTERED

4 POUNDS BABY BOK CHOY, CUT INTO 1/2-INCH SLICES, RINSED, AND DRIED

1 CUP SUN-DRIED TOMATOES

2 TABLESPOONS SOY SAUCE

1 TABLESPOON CRUSHED RED PEPPER (OPTIONAL)

1. In a 12-inch sauté pan or large wok, heat the oil over medium-high heat. Stir-fry the onion and garlic until the onion is translucent, about 2 minutes.

2. Add the scallops and cook for 3 minutes. Add the remaining ingredients and cook several minutes more, until the bok choy is wilted.

NOTE: If you do not have a large sauté pan, use 2 smaller pans rather than crowding one pan.

VARIATIONS

✦ Substitute 18 large shrimp, 12 ounces tempeh, or firm 12 ounces tofu for the scallops.

✦ Add a few thinly sliced shiitake mushrooms with the onions.

✦ Add 1 teaspoon minced fresh ginger with the onions.

BROILED ORANGES
WITH HONEY YOGURT AND PISTACHIOS

❋ SERVES 6 ❋

Winter citrus brings a taste of the sun during cold, gray days. Don't limit your enjoyment to juices or salads; warming citrus lifts it to a new, sweet dimension. A quick run under the broiler gets the honey bubbling and the juice from the oranges makes a wonderful sauce to mingle with thick, creamy yogurt. Sweet red grapefruit, mandarin oranges, tangerines, or clementines (or a combination of these) would be equally delicious.

2 CUPS THICK GREEK-STYLE PLAIN YOGURT, *LABNA* (PAGE 60)

5 LARGE ORANGES

A FEW DROPS OF ORANGE FLOWER WATER OR ROSE WATER (SEE NOTE)

1/4 CUP DARK THYME OR MESQUITE HONEY

3 TABLESPOONS CHOPPED PISTACHIOS

1. One day ahead of time, drain the yogurt. Set up a strainer over a bowl. Set a paper coffee filter in the strainer and pour the yogurt into the filter. Refrigerate for 24 hours; the yogurt will be very thick.

2. Preheat the broiler on high.

3. With a zester, remove the thin orange skin in long strips from 1 orange. (You may also use a peeler and then cut the pieces into long thin strips.) Set aside.

4. Working over a plate to catch the juices, cut off the top and bottom of the orange with a sharp knife. Then cut the peel away from top to bottom, following the curved shape of the fruit. Peel the remaining oranges in this way.

5. Slice the peeled fruit into ½-inch-thick rounds and place in a single, slightly overlapping layer in a shallow baking dish. (Use 2 dishes if needed rather than overcrowding one.) Sprinkle with orange flower water and any juices from the oranges. Drizzle ⅛ cup of the honey over the oranges. Broil close to the element until the honey is bubbly hot, 2 to 3 minutes. The fruit will not brown.

6. While the oranges are under the broiler, whisk the remaining ⅛ cup of honey and the yogurt in a small bowl.

7. Divide the orange slices evenly among 6 small plates. Spoon any juices from the baking dish over the oranges, and top with honey yogurt, a few strips of orange zest, and some pistachios.

NOTE: There is a subtle flavor of the Near East here, with distilled flower essences, bright-green pistachios, and *labna*, thickened yogurt. Flower water is sold at Middle Eastern markets. It is very potent—a few small drops is enough to perfume the oranges.

VARIATIONS

✦ Jesús sometimes glazes orange slices with agave syrup and sears them quickly in a hot pan or on the grill.

✦ Use agave or maple syrup instead of honey.

✦ Crème fraîche may be substituted for the yogurt. There is no need to drain it.

LA POSADA

✦

PONCHE

TOSTADITAS WITH AZTEC GUACAMOLE AND CUCUMBER-JICAMA SALSA

SHRIMP ENCHILADAS WITH PICANTE SAUCE

FRIJOLES COLORADO DE LA OLLA WITH GUAJILLO CHILE

MEXICAN RED RICE

VANILLA BEAN FLAN WITH AGAVE SYRUP AND CARAMELIZED WALNUTS

CHOCOLATE CHIP–CRANBERRY COOKIES

✦

In a culture that celebrates the family, La Posada is the ultimate family occasion, a re-enactment of the wanderings of the Virgin Mary and Joseph as they sought shelter for the birth of their son. From mid-December until Christmas Eve, groups of revelers go door to door in their immediate neighborhood singing songs and asking for la posada. *At each door they are turned away until at the end of the evening the host family (a different one each night) invites everyone inside for the inevitable fiesta.*

PONCHE

❀ MAKES 1 GALLON ❀

During the Posada in December, a pot of *ponche* is always simmering on the stove to warm up chilly guests. The punch is usually served with a few bits of fruit but may be strained if you prefer. Serve in heatproof cups or mugs, with sticks of cinnamon. Adults may enjoy the addition of a drop of tequila or rum.

2 GREEN APPLES, CORED AND CUT INTO 8 PIECES EACH

1 ORANGE, CUT INTO 8 PIECES

1 LEMON, CUT INTO 8 PIECES

3 THICK SLICES FRESH PINEAPPLE, PEELED, CORED, AND CUT INTO LARGE CHUNKS

TWO 6-INCH PIECES SUGARCANE, PEELED AND CUT INTO 1-INCH PIECES

¼ CUP SEEDLESS RAISINS

1 CUP SUGAR, OR MORE TO TASTE

4 LARGE CINNAMON STICKS

2 PIECES STAR ANISE

8 TEJOCOTE (MEXICAN HAWTHORN APPLES) OR DRIED APPLE RINGS

10 CUPS COLD WATER

In a large pot, combine all of the ingredients and bring to a simmer over low heat. Cover and simmer for about 1 hour or until the punch is flavorful. Taste and add more sugar if you prefer.

TOSTADITAS WITH AZTEC GUACAMOLE AND CUCUMBER-JICAMA SALSA

❀ SERVES 6 ❀

No fiesta is complete without crisp *tostaditas* served with various salsas and guacamole for dipping. These are baked, not fried, with a small amount of olive oil from a handy spray bottle. Serve a platter of raw vegetables alongside. This time of year, celery, carrots, jicama, sweet bell peppers, cauliflower, and broccoli, served with some cut limes, are good choices. Baked chips may soften overnight, so refresh any leftovers with a quick turn in a hot oven.

24 THIN WHITE CORN TORTILLAS

OLIVE OIL IN A SPRAY BOTTLE

SEA SALT

AZTEC GUACAMOLE (PAGE 90)

CUCUMBER-JICAMA SALSA (RECIPE FOLLOWS)

1. Preheat the oven to 325 degrees F.

2. Cut the tortillas into 4 or 6 wedges and toss them in a bowl while spraying with olive oil.

3. Spread in a single layer on baking sheets, salt lightly, and bake until crisp and golden brown, about 20 minutes, stirring once and turning the pan.

4. Serve with guacamole and salsa.

CUCUMBER-JICAMA SALSA

❀ MAKES 1 1/4 CUPS ❀

1 ROMA TOMATO, CUT INTO 1/2-INCH DICE

1/2 SMALL SERRANO CHILE, SEEDED AND MINCED

1/2 CUP DICED PEELED CUCUMBER

1/2 CUP DICED PEELED JICAMA (1/2 SMALL JICAMA)

1/4 CUP CILANTRO, MINCED

1/3 CUP THINLY SLICED GREEN ONIONS

JUICE OF 1 LIME (ABOUT 2 TABLE-SPOONS), OR MORE TO TASTE

1/4 TEASPOON SEA SALT, OR MORE TO TASTE

1/8 TEASPOON FRESH GROUND BLACK PEPPER

Combine all ingredients in a medium bowl. Add more lime juice and salt to taste.

NOTE: Your salsa bar could be stretched to include Pico de Gallo (page 89), Tres Estrellas Salsa (page 28), and Mango Salsa (page 91).

SHRIMP ENCHILADAS
WITH PICANTE SAUCE

❁ SERVES 6 ❁

Enchiladas are simply corn tortillas dipped in a chile-rich sauce and rolled around any kind of filling. This shrimp enchilada is typical of the Tecate region, which is only a short drive from the coast. It is simple and quick to make; most of the ingredients are fresh vegetables.

Take the preparation in steps. The Ancho Chile Salsa and Picante Sauce can be made two days ahead, the cutting and dicing of ingredients can be done another day, the filling can be made and the whole dish assembled the day before the party. Wild Mexican shrimp from the Gulf of California would be used in Mexico, but any large shrimp (preferably wild) will do. They are great on a buffet—cut the enchiladas in half before serving, so everyone can taste, or double or triple the recipe to serve a crowd.

1 TEASPOON OLIVE OIL

3 CLOVES GARLIC, PEELED AND MINCED (ABOUT 1 TABLESPOON)

1/4 RED ONION, PEELED AND CUT INTO 1/4-INCH DICE (ABOUT 1/2 CUP)

1/2 POUND LARGE SHRIMP, SHELLED, DEVEINED, AND CUT INTO 6 PIECES EACH

1/2 SMALL RED BELL PEPPER, SEEDED AND CUT INTO 1/4-INCH DICE

1/2 SMALL GREEN OR YELLOW BELL PEPPER, SEEDED AND CUT INTO 1/4-INCH DICE

1 SMALL KOHLRABI, PEELED AND CUT INTO 1/4-INCH DICE, OR 1 STALK CELERY, CUT INTO 1/4-INCH DICE

2 CUPS SPINACH OR OTHER DARK LEAFY GREENS, SHREDDED

1 TEASPOON SEA SALT

1/4 TEASPOON FRESH GROUND BLACK PEPPER

1/4 CUP FRESH CILANTRO LEAVES, ROUGHLY CHOPPED

1/2 TEASPOON CHOPPED FRESH OREGANO LEAVES

2 OUNCES GRATED JACK CHEESE (ABOUT 1/2 CUP)

ANCHO CHILE SALSA (PAGE 39)

12 CORN TORTILLAS

1/4 CUP CRUMBLED DRY COTIJA CHEESE

1/4 CUP CREMA FRESCA, CRÈME FRAÎCHE, OR SOUR CREAM

PICANTE SAUCE (PAGE 91)

1. Pre-heat oven to 350 degrees F.

2. In a 10-inch sauté pan, heat the olive oil over medium heat. Sauté the garlic and onion for about 1 minute. Add the shrimp and cook, stirring constantly, until it turns pink. Add the peppers, kohlrabi, and spinach. Season with salt and black pepper and continue to cook another 5 minutes, stirring often. Stir in the cilantro and oregano and cool completely before stirring in 1/4 cup of Jack cheese.

3. Spread 1/3 cup of the Salsa in the bottom of an 11 × 9-inch baking dish.

4. Heat a heavy griddle over medium-high heat. Warm a tortilla briefly on both sides until it softens. Place 3 tablespoons of the shrimp filling onto a tortilla and roll up. Set seam-side down in the baking dish. Repeat with the remaining tortillas, tucking them close together in the dish.

5. Spoon the rest of the salsa over the enchiladas, sprinkle evenly with the remaining 1/4 cup of Jack cheese and the cotija cheese, and bake until very hot, about 20 minutes.

6. Stir the crema fresca with a fork until smooth, and drizzle over the enchiladas for a traditional finish. (Sour cream may have to be thinned with 1 teaspoon of water.) Serve the Picante Sauce on the side.

ESSENTIAL MEXICAN TASTES

These are the essential tastes of Mexico: toasted corn, dried chiles, charred vegetables, and richly flavored beans, set off with the freshness and spice of tomato, lime, cilantro, hot chiles, sweet onions, and fruit. In his classes at La Cocina, Jesús draws on authentic Mexican tastes and the bounty of Tres Estrellas to create innovative cooking that's both good for you and soul-satisfying.

One of the world's most ancient foodways, Mexican cooking is based on corn, beans, and plenty of fresh vegetables used inventively. Mexican cuisine is inherently healthy as well as delicious. Meat and other proteins are used in small amounts relative to other ingredients. Consider the American archetype of a large slab of grilled meat or fish on a plate with plenty of starch and one or two cooked vegetables. Now contrast that with a plate of small tacos in fresh corn tortillas, topped with fresh raw salsas made of vitamin-packed fresh vegetables. Other common ingredients, like hard squash and dried chiles, are nutritional powerhouses. Instead of sodas or caloric coffee drinks, Mexicans drink *aguas frescas* (page 34) made from fresh fruit and water, and prefer ripe fruit to elaborate sweets.

FRIJOLES COLORADO DE LA OLLA WITH GUAJILLO CHILE

❋ MAKES ABOUT 4 CUPS ❋

These pinto beans, cooked until creamy and almost falling apart, are richly flavored with mild chiles, onion, and garlic. The recipe may be doubled or tripled.

1 CUP SMALL DRIED PINTO BEANS

5 TO 6 CUPS VEGETABLE STOCK (PAGE 176)

2 BAY LEAVES

1 *GUAJILLO* CHILE, SEEDED AND TORN INTO SMALL PIECES

2 TABLESPOONS EXTRA-VIRGIN OLIVE OIL

1 1/2 CUPS CHOPPED ONION

1/2 TEASPOON CRUSHED RED PEPPER

1/2 TEASPOON SEA SALT

1. In a large saucepan, soak the beans overnight in enough water to cover. In the morning, drain the water and rinse the beans. Drain again.

2. Return the beans to the saucepan and add the stock, bay leaves, and guajillo. Bring the beans to a boil, reduce the heat to low, cover, and simmer until tender, about 2 hours. Add more water or stock as needed to cover the beans.

3. In a sauté pan, heat the olive oil over medium heat for five minutes. Add the onion and sauté until the onions are translucent. Add the red pepper and salt.

4. Mix the onions with the beans and cook over low heat for 15 minutes. Discard the guajillo pieces before serving.

VARIATIONS

✦ Substitute small red beans or black beans for the pintos.

✦ Mash the beans and serve hot, with a sprinkling of cotija cheese.

MICROWAVES

Founder Deborah loathes microwaves and won't have one in her kitchen. In her opinion, microwaving is not cooking. She wants cooks to get in touch with food through the slow food approach of touching, stirring, adjusting the heat . . . actual cooking, as opposed to reheating.

MEXICAN RED RICE

❋ SERVES 6 ❋

Rice rounds out most meals in Mexico and is usually cooked with vegetables and a touch of tomato.

1 TEASPOON OLIVE OIL

1/2 SMALL WHITE ONION, PEELED
AND CUT INTO 1/4-INCH DICE
(ABOUT 1/2 CUP)

1 CLOVE GARLIC, PEELED AND MINCED

1/2 SMALL GREEN BELL PEPPER OR
ANAHEIM CHILE, SEEDED AND CUT
INTO 1/4-INCH DICE

1/4 CUP MINCED CARROT

1 TEASPOON GROUND CALIFORNIA
CHILE

1 CUP LONG-GRAIN BROWN RICE

1 TEASPOON SEA SALT

1 MEDIUM TOMATO PUREED WITH
2 CUPS WATER

1/2 CUP COOKED GREEN PEAS OR
COOKED EDAMAME (OPTIONAL)

1. In a 2-quart saucepan, heat the olive oil over medium heat. Cook the onions, garlic, green pepper, and carrot for 5 minutes, stirring often. Add the rice, chile, and salt and cook for 1 minute.

2. Add the tomato puree to the pan and bring to a boil. Cover the pan and reduce the heat to low. Simmer for 40 minutes, or until all the liquid is absorbed.

3. Remove from heat. Fluff the rice with a fork and stir in the peas if desired. Replace the lid and let the rice steam for 10 minutes.

ROASTED GARLIC EN CAZUELA

Pack any number of trimmed garlic heads into a baking dish (cazuela) just large enough to hold them. Pour some good olive oil over the top, season with salt, pepper, and fresh thyme sprigs. Cover loosely with foil and bake at 325 degrees F until soft and buttery. Reserve the oil for cooking.

For smaller quantities, roast whole peeled cloves in foil or in a ramekin of olive oil.

VANILLA BEAN FLAN WITH AGAVE SYRUP AND CARAMELIZED WALNUTS

❋ SERVES 6 ❋

This light custard has a silky texture and is delicately flavored with vanilla bean and the light sweetness of agave syrup and toasted walnuts. It will melt in your mouth. Serve with a couple of crunchy caramelized walnuts and fresh fruit or poached dried fruit on the side.

1 1/2 CUPS MILK

1 FRESH VANILLA BEAN OR 1 TABLESPOON VANILLA EXTRACT

3 EXTRA-LARGE EGGS, PLUS 2 EGG YOLKS

1/2 CUP FIRMLY PACKED DARK BROWN SUGAR

4 TABLESPOONS DARK AGAVE SYRUP

6 TABLESPOONS CHOPPED CARAMELIZED WALNUTS

SEASONAL FRESH FRUIT OR POACHED DRIED FRUIT (OPTIONAL)

CARAMELIZED WALNUTS

1 CUP WALNUT HALVES, CHOPPED

2 TABLESPOONS AGAVE SYRUP, MAPLE SYRUP, OR HONEY

1 TABLESPOON BROWN SUGAR

1. Preheat the oven to 350 degrees F.

2. Pour the milk into a 2-quart heavy-bottomed saucepan. Split the vanilla bean and, with the tip of a sharp knife, scrape all the black paste from the bean into the milk. Add the pod. Heat the milk over medium heat until the milk is very hot and bubbles form around the edges of the pan, but do not allow it to boil. Remove from the heat and let stand 5 minutes.

3. Break the eggs into a mixing bowl, add the egg yolks and brown sugar and mix thoroughly. Slowly add 1 cup of the hot milk to the eggs, whisking as you pour; this tempers the eggs. Add the rest of the hot milk a little at a time to make a custard.

4. Strain the custard back into the pan through a coarse sieve, and carefully skim off any foam. Scrape the vanilla specks out of the sieve and return them to the custard.

5. Put 2 teaspoons of syrup in the bottom of each of six 6-ounce straight-sided ovenproof ramekins. Chill for 15 minutes to thicken the syrup. Pouring carefully, divide the custard evenly among the ramekins.

6. Place the ramekins in a baking pan. Carefully pour 1 inch of boiling water into the pan, being careful not to splash water into the custard. Cover with foil and bake on the middle rack of the oven for approximately 30 to 35 minutes, or until the custards are no longer jiggly in the centers.

7. Remove from the oven, take off the foil, and let the custards cool in the water-filled pan. When cool, remove the ramekins from the pan, cover, and refrigerate for up to 48 hours.

8. For the caramelized walnuts, lower the oven heat to 300 degrees F. In a small bowl, toss the walnuts with the agave syrup until lightly and evenly coated. Place the nuts in a single layer on a lightly oiled baking sheet. Roast until lightly browned, about 5 to 7 minutes. Check them frequently to be sure they are not burning. Spread out on wax paper to cool. Store cooled nuts.

9. To serve, top each custard with 1 tablespoon of walnuts and some fruit, if desired.

CHOCOLATE CHIP–CRANBERRY COOKIES

❋ MAKES 4 DOZEN ❋

Friday is eagerly anticipated Cookie Day at the Ranch. The lucky staff member who walks around with the basket, handing out cookie bliss, is the recipient of many a heartfelt *¡gracias!* Who wouldn't be happy? Each cookie is packed with tart cranberries and chewy, crisp oats and has a fat chocolate *beso* in the middle. Although made with healthy grains, these are real cookies, so keep them small and enjoy in moderation.

1 CUP UNSALTED BUTTER, SOFTENED

1/2 CUP FIRMLY PACKED BROWN SUGAR

2 EGGS

1 CUP MILK

2 CUPS ROLLED OATS

1 CUP WHEAT GERM

1 CUP WHEAT FLAKE CEREAL

1 CUP WHITE WHOLE-WHEAT FLOUR OR WHOLE-WHEAT PASTRY FLOUR

1 CUP SLICED ALMONDS

1 TEASPOON CINNAMON

1 TEASPOON BAKING POWDER

1/2 TEASPOON BAKING SODA

1 CUP SEMISWEET CHOCOLATE CHIPS

1/2 CUP DRIED CRANBERRIES, CHOPPED

CHOCOLATE KISSES, UNWRAPPED

1. Preheat the oven to 350 degrees F.

2. In a stand mixer fitted with the paddle attachment, cream the butter and brown sugar. Add the eggs one at a time, then the milk, beating until combined. (The milk will not quite combine with the butter or the mixture will look a little separated, but this is fine.)

3. In a separate bowl, combine the oats, wheat germ, cereal, pastry flour, almonds, cinnamon, baking powder, and baking soda. Add the chocolate chips and cranberries.

4. Add oat mixture to the milk mixture, and mix on the lowest speed until thoroughly combined. Use a tablespoon measure or small ice cream scoop to scoop the dough onto lightly oiled baking sheets, leaving 2 inches between each scoop. Press a chocolate kiss into the center of each cookie. Bake for 14 minutes, or until lightly browned.

New Year's Eve

✦

ROASTED PEAR AND ARUGULA SALAD
WITH POMEGRANATE-CHIPOTLE VINAIGRETTE

LOBSTER A LA DIABLA

POTATO-KOHLRABI GRATIN WITH GARLIC AND WHITE TRUFFLE OIL

MIDNIGHT DUET:
CHOCOLATE CAKE WITH ALMONDS *AND*
MAYAN CHOCOLATE SORBET

✦

*The turning of the year calls for something special, like lobster and truffles.
From the tangy pomegranate salad to the elegant dessert duet, everything
on this menu is light, sophisticated, and easy to do—and tastes sensational.
Much of the preparation may be done well ahead of time.*

ROASTED PEAR AND ARUGULA SALAD WITH POMEGRANATE-CHIPOTLE VINAIGRETTE

❉ SERVES 6 ❉

Pomegranates, an old fruit with a new following, appear in the market starting in November. Older varieties are ruby-red, sour-tart, and full of flavor. Pomegranate juice—an antioxidant par excellence—is readily available year round and serves as the base for the vinaigrette, but do add some fresh pomegranate seeds to the salad if they are available. The small amount of chipotle in the dressing is not hot but gives a hint of smokiness that is wonderful with the sweet pear.

6 SMALL PEARS

1 TABLESPOON AGAVE SYRUP

4 CUPS BABY ARUGULA, STEMMED AND WASHED

2 CUPS MIXED BABY LETTUCES, WITH SOME RED COLOR, STEMMED AND WASHED

POMEGRANATE SEEDS (OPTIONAL)

POMEGRANATE-CHIPOTLE VINAIGRETTE

1 SMALL CLOVE GARLIC, PEELED AND MINCED

1 MEDIUM SHALLOT, PEELED AND MINCED

³/4 CUP STRONG, UNSWEETENED POMEGRANATE JUICE

2 TABLESPOONS RED WINE VINEGAR

1¹/2 TABLESPOONS BROWN SUGAR

1 TABLESPOONS EXTRA-VIRGIN OLIVE OIL

2 TEASPOONS ORANGE ZEST

¹/8 TEASPOON SEA SALT

¹/8 TEASPOON FRESH GROUND BLACK PEPPER

PINCH OF GROUND CLOVES

¹/8 TEASPOON GROUND DRIED CHIPOTLE OR CHIPOTLE IN ADOBO, OR MORE TO TASTE

1. Preheat the oven to 350 degrees F.

2. Core the pears from the bottom, using a small spoon or melon baller. You may peel them or not, but leave the stem intact. Brush the pears with the agave syrup and roast on a baking sheet until browned and tender, 30 to 45 minutes depending on the size and ripeness of the pears.

3. Whisk all the vinaigrette ingredients together or puree in a blender.

4. To serve, combine the baby arugula and lettuces with the dressing and divide among 6 chilled plates. Set a pear on each plate and scatter some pomegranate seeds on the greens, if desired. Pass the extra dressing separately.

VARIATIONS

✦ Add crumbled feta or blue cheese and Caramelized Walnuts (page 154).

✦ Substitute small apples for the pears.

LOBSTER A LA DIABLA

※ SERVES 6 ※

Since he is a professional chef, Jesús is often called upon to cook for his large extended family on holidays. This recipe is his hands-down favorite. His family adores the spicy sauce, which sparkles with fresh lime juice; Jesús likes it because it takes about 10 minutes to cook from start to finish, with very little preparation time. The *a la diabla* sauce is commonly served with seafood all over Baja California. It is a little spicy, but not overwhelmingly so, and you may reduce the amount of hot chile or eliminate it altogether. It will still be delicious.

When cooking for a small group, it's best to have all the ingredients ready to cook as soon as the salad is cleared. The method of cooking is a true restaurant-style sauté, which goes quickly. The dish is best served immediately, but the finished *diabla* can also be held in a chafing dish over low heat for up to 30 minutes. Should you wish to double the recipe, cook in two batches rather than one large one.

Any kind of lobster or langoustine may be used. Cooking in the split shell improves the flavor, but you may certainly remove the meat from the shell before cooking. This recipe is also excellent with large shrimp, scallops, cracked crab legs, mussels, or clams.

1 TABLESPOON OLIVE OIL

6 LARGE LOBSTER TAILS, IN THE SHELL, SPLIT IN HALF

1 CUP VERY THINLY SLICED LEEKS, WHITE PART ONLY

¼ CUP FRESH GARLIC (ABOUT 8 LARGE CLOVES)

⅓ CUP FRESH LIME JUICE

1 TABLESPOON CHOPPED CHIPOTLES IN ADOBO, OR SAMBAL PASTE (SEE NOTE)

¼ CUP 100 PERCENT AGAVE TEQUILA

1 CUP DICED TOMATOES

1 CUP FRESH CILANTRO, CHOPPED (1 SMALL BUNCH)

2 TABLESPOONS BUTTER (OPTIONAL)

1. In a 12-inch sauté pan, heat the olive oil over medium-high heat. If you don't have a large sauté pan, use two 10-inch pans.

2. Add the lobster tails and cook, stirring, until they start to turn pink—about 2 minutes. Add the leeks and garlic and cook, stirring, for 1 minute.

3. Add the lime juice and shake the pan to combine. When the lime juice begins to boil, add the chipotles and stir to combine.

4. Remove the pan from the heat and pour in the tequila. Return to the burner and bring to a boil. Cook until the sauce begins to thicken, about 2 minutes, then reduce the heat slightly. Add the tomatoes and cilantro, stir, then add the butter, stirring just until the butter melts. Serve as soon as possible.

NOTE: Sambal paste is available at Asian groceries.

POTATO-KOHLRABI GRATIN WITH GARLIC AND WHITE TRUFFLE OIL

❉ SERVES 6 ❉

A gratin is simply thin slices of vegetables, laid in a shallow dish in neat overlapping rows, and baked with stock or cream until lightly browned. Here, firm waxy potatoes alternate with layers of thinly sliced kohlrabi, an uncommon vegetable that deserves much wider appreciation. Despite its odd looks, kohlrabi tastes a bit like nuts and a bit like sweet celery. It is available from fall through late winter. Truffles are a natural best friend to potatoes and garlic, and while it sounds extravagant, a little truffle oil goes a long way. This creamy gratin creates the perfect balance for the spicy lobster sauce.

3 LARGE RED POTATOES, SCRUBBED BUT NOT PEELED

1 KOHLRABI, TRIMMED AND PEELED

1 TABLESPOON EXTRA-VIRGIN OLIVE OIL

1 LEEK, WHITE PART ONLY, WASHED AND THINLY SLICED

4 CLOVES GARLIC, PEELED AND THINLY SLICED

1½ TO 2 CUPS BASIC VEGETABLE STOCK (PAGE 176)

1 TEASPOON SEA SALT

FRESH GROUND BLACK PEPPER

2 OUNCES PARMESAN CHEESE, FINELY GRATED (ABOUT ½ CUP)

1 TEASPOON WHITE TRUFFLE OIL OR FRUITY EXTRA-VIRGIN OLIVE OIL

1. Preheat the oven to 350 degrees F.

2. With a mandoline or sharp knife, thinly slice the potatoes and kohlrabi and place the slices in a bowl of cold water to prevent browning.

3. Drizzle the olive oil over the bottom of a shallow, 11 × 9-inch gratin or baking dish. Set aside 1 tablespoon of the leek, then evenly scatter one-third of the remaining leek and one-third of the garlic over the olive oil.

4. Top with one-third of the sliced potatoes and kohlrabi, slightly overlapping the slices to form a neat, even layer. Moisten the potatoes with a small amount of stock. Sprinkle with a pinch of salt and a grind of pepper. Sprinkle one-third of the grated cheese evenly over the potatoes.

5. Top the cheese with half of the remaining leeks and garlic and continue in the same way with the potatoes, kohlrabi, stock, salt, pepper, and cheese. Repeat once more, ending with a carefully arranged layer of potatoes and kohlrabi. Top with the reserved leeks.

6. Pour the remaining stock carefully around the edges of the gratin; the dish will look juicy. Bake for about 1 hour, or until the potatoes are tender when pierced with a knife and the top is lightly browned. If it looks as though the potatoes are drying out at any time during the cooking, add a small amount of stock around the edges. There should still be a small amount of liquid in the dish when the gratin is done.

7. Just before serving, drizzle the white truffle oil evenly over the top of the gratin.

VARIATIONS

✦ Peeled zucchini, hard squash, celery root, or sweet potatoes may be substituted for the kohlrabi.

✦ Add a thin layer of greens (such as spinach, kale, or chard) to the gratin.

MIDNIGHT DUET:
CHOCOLATE CAKE WITH ALMONDS

❋ SERVES 6 ❋

This dense, ultra-chocolatey cake is baked with an upside-down layer of slivered almonds and more chocolate. A small piece of cake topped with a scoop of cinnamon-scented Mayan Chocolate Sorbet is a perfect pairing.

For a garnish, consider seasonal citrus, such as sliced oranges or tangerines, or the tiny kumquat. Slice a few pieces of citrus to scatter around the plate and add a sprig of mint. If you have frozen summer berries on hand, puree them into a lightly sweetened sauce, or consider pomegranate seeds, quince *mermelada* (see page 109), or poached dried figs and apricots cooked with a little orange liqueur.

½ CUP MILK

1 CUP SEMISWEET CHOCOLATE CHIPS

½ CUP SLICED ALMONDS, LIGHTLY TOASTED

3 EGGS, BEATEN

⅓ CUP FIRMLY PACKED BROWN SUGAR

½ CUP SOUR CREAM

½ CUP ALL-PURPOSE FLOUR

½ CUP COCOA POWDER

2 TEASPOONS BAKING SODA

¼ CUP POWDERED SUGAR (OPTIONAL)

1. Preheat the oven to 350 degrees F.

2. In a small saucepan, gently heat the milk over medium-low heat until warm, about 2 minutes. Remove from the heat and stir in ½ cup of the chocolate chips. Stir until the chips are melted and the mixture is smooth.

3. Lightly butter an 8-cup cake pan or 8 × 8-inch baking dish, and line the bottom with a piece of parchment cut to fit. Spread the almonds and the remaining ½ cup chocolate chips evenly over the parchment.

4. Whisk the eggs and brown sugar together until well combined. Whisk in the sour cream and set aside.

5. Sift together the flour, cocoa powder, and baking soda, and stir into the eggs until just combined. Pour into the prepared pan and bake for

30 minutes, or until a toothpick or skewer inserted in the center comes out clean.

6. Run a knife around the outside edge and remove the cake from the pan by turning it upside down on a rack. Cool the cake completely.

7. Cut the cake into thin slices to serve. Top each serving with a small scoop of sorbet and a dusting of powdered sugar, if desired.

VARIATIONS

✦ Jesús often substitutes buckwheat flour for some or all of the all-purpose flour, which results in a softer texture.

✦ Several hours before serving, brush the cake with a mixture of 2 tablespoons agave syrup and 1 tablespoon of a liqueur of your choice, such as amaretto, Grand Marnier, Kahlua, or dark rum.

MAYAN CHOCOLATE SORBET

❦ MAKES 4 CUPS ❦

Chocolate (*xocolatl*) was originally developed by the Mayan people of southern Mexico, long before the Spanish conquest. This creamy sorbet is based on an authentic Mexican drink recipe and has a secret ingredient.

Dark chocolate in small quantities offers real health benefits. This suits Jesús fine; he loves chocolate and always has Chocolate Banana Bread (page 133) or something gooey tucked in the refrigerator for an afternoon pick-me-up.

1 CUP COOKED BUTTERNUT SQUASH PULP

3½ CUPS MILK

3 OUNCES IBARRA BRAND MEXICAN CHOCOLATE

3 OUNCES SEMISWEET CHOCOLATE, CHOPPED

½ TEASPOON GROUND CINNAMON

½ TEASPOON GROUND CARDAMOM

⅛ TEASPOON FRESHLY GRATED NUTMEG

1. In a blender, puree the squash with 1¾ cups of the milk until perfectly smooth.

2. In a large saucepan, mix the remaining 1¾ cups of milk, chocolate, and spices. With a whisk, stir over low heat until the chocolate is melted, then add the pureed squash. Do not boil. Strain through a coarse sieve to remove any trace of the squash fiber.

3. Cool at room temperature, stirring occasionally, then chill completely.

4. Freeze in an ice cream maker according to manufacturer's directions, or see page 125 for an alternate method.

VARIATION

✦ In chilly weather serve the same recipe as a hot drink, in little demitasse cups, with a crisp cookie for dipping.

BASICS

Students at La Cocina Que Canta have expert teachers on hand to answer questions and offer suggestions. This chapter is your everyday reference for quick inspiration, essential information, cooking techniques, and tips to make you a better and more confident cook. Think you're too busy to make a healthy meal? Check this chapter for ideas for quick dinners using what you have on hand in your well-stocked pantry. Here you will find directions on how to transform your favorite recipes into healthy meals and how to cook staples such as grains, rice, and beans. Our hope is that you feel you have a great teacher right there beside you in the kitchen.

GRAINS

Delicious whole grains are the ancient foundation for a healthy diet. They make a satisfying meal on their own when topped with cooked vegetables or cheese. Whole grains are as quick and easy to cook as rice, but are a more potent source of important vitamins, minerals, and protein as well as essential complex carbohydrates. Use whole grains as you would rice, as a side dish or as a base for a main course. Most grains firm up after cooling, making them suitable for use in salads. Buy organic whole grains in small quantities and store in the freezer.

BARLEY   Barley is the oldest cultivated grain. It stays chewy when cooked and has a mild flavor. It makes excellent salads, stuffing, or side dishes, or can be added to the cooked grains in Market Vegetable Soup (page 122).

BUCKWHEAT   Native to Asia and widely used in Russia (as buckwheat groats or kasha), buckwheat has a mildly bitter taste. Try adding it to sautéed onions, apples, and black pepper for a savory side dish.

BULGUR   Bulgur is whole-wheat kernels that have been cooked, dried, and broken up. Quick-cooking bulgur is nutty, chewy, sweet, and high in protein. Use hot as a side dish, or use in a salad, such as tabbouleh (see Black Quinoa Tabbouleh, page 64).

COUSCOUS   Couscous is made from wheat flour that has been moistened and rolled into tiny pellets. It looks and cooks like a grain. Whole-wheat couscous will be ready to eat in less than 2 minutes, and it carries flavors beautifully.

CORN   Dried ground corn may be purchased in the form of grits or polenta. Always choose the coarsest grind. A small amount of Parmesan cheese may be stirred in at the end of cooking, or add chopped sun-dried tomatoes, garlic, or caramelized onions.

FARRO   An ancient form of wheat popular in Italy, farro has a delicious flavor and a chewy texture similar to barley. Try combining it with dried fruit and nuts or herbs (see Tuscan Farro Salad, page 26). It is very high in B vitamins. Barley may be substituted for farro in most recipes.

MILLET   This tiny grain is widely used in China, Africa, and India. It is soft when cooked, with separate grains, and has a mild taste. Cooked millet is best served warm combined with another grain or an exotic rice.

QUINOA   The tough little quinoa plant is native to South America. The small, pearly grains are rich in quality protein. It looks light and fluffy like couscous when cooked and has a chewy grain with a little yellow "tail." The flavor is mild but distinct enough to stand up on its own. Two types are available: black quinoa and white. They may be used interchangeably. Quinoa is delicious served hot or cold.

WHEAT BERRIES   Berries are whole unprocessed kernels of grain and are very hard. Wheat berries are the most commonly used, but berries of triticale or rye are also available. They must be soaked and cooked for a long period of time; even then, they are too chewy to eat on their own. Instead, add to salads or combine with another grain or rice, or add to a batch of bread. Before cooking, combine the berries with water (see page 168) and bring to a boil. Turn off the heat and let soak for 1 hour. Berries may also be soaked overnight in a large thermos filled with boiling water.

HOW TO ADD WHOLE GRAINS TO YOUR EVERYDAY COOKING

It's easy to modify your favorite recipes to include more healthy whole grains.

+ Substitute whole-wheat flour for half of the white flour in existing recipes.

+ Substitute other types of whole grain flour, such as buckwheat or ground oats for one-quarter of the white flour in recipes for a different flavor and texture.

+ Add cooked grains or rolled grain cereal to your recipes for muffins, quick breads, scones, pancakes, cookies, or bread. Adding cooked rye and wheat berries to Ranch Flaxseed Bread (page 114) is delicious.

+ Mix equal amounts of cooked grains and rice to serve as a side dish.

+ Sprinkle cooked grains on salads

+ Substitute cooked grains in your favorite pasta or rice salad recipe.

+ Add cooked grains to soups and stuffings.

+ Use whole grains instead of rice to make a barley risotto, quinoa with sofrito, and so on.

HOW TO COOK GRAINS

Use a small, heavy-bottomed saucepan or stockpot with a tight-fitting lid to cook grains. Add filtered water or, for more flavor, Basic Vegetable Stock (page 176), and a pinch of salt, if desired. Bring the liquid to a boil and sprinkle in the grains (they will cook up fluffy and separate from one another). Shake the pan gently once or twice to evenly distribute the grain, cover, and reduce the heat to medium-low. During cooking, you can peek, but not too often, and do not stir the grain at any time.

When the water is absorbed, turn off the heat, fluff the grain gently with a fork, and cover the pan again to allow the grain to steam and finish absorbing any liquid. Leftover cooked grain should be refrigerated; all varieties reheat beautifully and may even be frozen.

GRAIN COOKING TIMES

	GRAIN	WATER	YIELD	COOKING TIME
BARLEY	1 cup	2 cups	3 1/2 cups	30 minutes
BUCKWHEAT	1 cup	1 1/2 cups	3 1/2 cups	10 minutes
BULGUR	1 cup	2 cups	3 1/2 cups	20 minutes
CORNMEAL	1 cup	3 3/4 cups	5 cups	45 minutes
COUSCOUS	1 cup	1 cup	2 cups	2 minutes
FARRO	1 cup	2 cups	3 cups	30 minutes
MILLET	1 cup	1 3/4 cups	3 1/2 cups	20 minutes
QUINOA	1 cup	1 1/3 cups	3 1/2 cups	15 minutes
WHEAT BERRIES	1/2 cup	2 cups	2 cups	1 hour

QUICK IDEAS FOR GRAINS

Grains lend themselves to almost infinite variation, depending on what you have on hand. In summer add fresh herbs and vegetables for cool salads; in winter, flavor with spices and stock or dried fruit and serve hot. Cooked grains reheat well and are a terrific base for leftovers (which we prefer to think of as cooking smart by planning and cooking ahead).

✦ Flavor with a bay leaf, different kinds of stock, or a pinch of dried herb mix.

CORN POLENTA

Bring the water to a boil, add 1 teaspoon olive oil and 1/4 teaspoon kosher salt. Stir in the ground corn and reduce the heat to low. Cook, stirring often, for 45 minutes. It will be very thick.

WORK SMART!

Cooking from scratch requires a little extra effort on your part, but probably not as much as you think. Here are some ideas to help make preparing healthy food quicker and easier.

✦ **Plan ahead.** Cook once for two meals. Double recipes and eat for two days or freeze half. This works especially well for casseroles, pie crust, and breads. When you chop onions or peel garlic, do a little extra and keep it in the fridge. Grilling vegetables? Cook extra and add to rice or pasta.

✦ **Shop for fresh food several times a week.** Going to the market will inspire you, even at the end of a long day, and you can quickly imagine a simple meal.

✦ **Keep basics in the freezer.** Vegetable stock, pesto, pre-portioned meat and seafood, and frozen berries all keep well in the freezer and can be ready to use in a relatively short amount of time.

✦ **Streamline your workspace.** Put away unused equipment, books, and décor. This is your space. If you have lots of tools you never use, put them away where they aren't in your way. Investing in fewer but quality tools and equipment, such as a good knife and several quality pots and pans, makes cooking easier and more pleasurable. Buy helpful gadgets: Eat a lot of rice? Invest in a rice cooker.

✦ **Help yourself.** Keep healthy snacks in the fridge, ready for nibbling—cut up fruit and raw vegetables, *agua fresca,* and *palletas*.

✦ **Join a cooking team.** Co-op cooking and group cooking is an emerging trend as informal groups of families or individuals alternate or share cooking duties.

◆ Enjoy whole cooked grains for breakfast—cook with raisins and a cinnamon stick and sweeten lightly with agave syrup.

◆ Stir in some sautéed or grilled vegetables as a great way to use small amounts of leftovers.

◆ Add raisins and chopped nuts or sunflower seeds and serve hot or cold.

◆ Add bright green cooked peas or edamame to cooked grains.

◆ Turn grains into a crunchy salad with diced tomatoes, cucumbers, herbs, and vinaigrette.

◆ Toast any grain slowly in a dry pan, then cook as directed and add caramelized onions and fresh thyme leaves.

◆ Sauté mushrooms with garlic and shallots and add to cooked grain.

◆ Add chopped fresh herbs, such as dill, chives, tarragon, thyme, or parsley.

◆ Add small pieces of sun-dried tomatoes and chopped basil.

◆ Add chopped cilantro, tomatoes, and a bit of hot serrano chile.

◆ Add roasted garlic (page 153).

◆ Add cooked wheat berries to a rice pilaf or cooked orzo pasta.

RICE

Try some of the many delicious colors and varieties of rice found in natural food stores and Asian markets. Rice, like grain, lends itself to endless experimentation with seasonings, additions, and cooking styles. See Quick Variations for Rice (page 174) for easy ideas to perk up your rice, and for some quick toppings. Generally, brown or whole grain rice is healthier and tastes better than white or polished rice, but takes longer to cook and may be stickier. Long-grain rice will be fluffier when cooked, and short-grain rice will be softer. Unlike grains, however, different types of rice require different cooking techniques. Read the rice description below, then refer to the cooking chart that follows for exact directions.

ARBORIO A very starchy short-grained rice that cooks up dense and creamy, arborio is used only for risotto and cannot be steamed or boiled.

BASMATI Basmati is a form of polished, specially aged white rice with very long, slender grains. This is the type of rice used for pilaf, but it can be steamed. It has a delicate perfume when cooked and is excellent with curries or Middle Eastern flavors.

BROWN Brown rice is whole-grain rice with the nutritious coating intact. It comes in both long-grain and short-grain varieties; the long-grain will be fluffy when cooked, the short-grain has a tendency to be sticky. (Brown rice can be steamed, or cooked pilaf-, paella-, or Mexican-style.)

CHINESE BLACK RICE Black rice is naturally sweet with a sticky and slightly glutinous texture. It is delicious for breakfast and should be cooked Japanese-style.

CONVERTED Converted rice is polished long-grain white rice that has been partially cooked, then dried. Converted rice stays firm and very fluffy when cooked. It can be steamed or cooked pilaf-, paella-, or Mexican-style.

EIGHT FAST RICE-BASED MEALS

Ranch founder Deborah Szekely considers her convenient rice cooker the essential piece of equipment in her kitchen. She starts her rice cooking, makes a quick side dish, and in less than 30 minutes is enjoying a hot meal.

With fresh-cooked rice ready, you've a good-for-you base for many quick, easy meals using whatever vegetables you have on hand. The quickest cooking techniques for vegetables are steaming, grilling, sautéing, pan-roasting, and stir-frying. (See Vegetables and Cooking Techniques, page 183.)

Even the simplest rice dish is improved by adding a sauce or flavoring from your well-stocked pantry, or a homemade salsa, chutney, or dressing. See the index for ideas. If you don't have a particular ingredient, don't be afraid to experiment—substitute whatever you have on hand and create a new favorite. Try serving these combinations over rice:

+ Diced tofu and leafy greens sautéed quickly with some green onions and a touch of hoisin sauce

+ Stir-fried scallops or vegetables and greens

+ Pan-roasted vegetables with fresh herbs and tomatoes

+ Mediterranean Saffron Stew with Lemon Zest Aioli (page 113)

+ Grilled vegetables with cilantro

+ Steamed vegetables with pesto or hummus

+ Fish baked on sliced tomatoes with a few shallots and a squeeze of lemon

+ Vegetables cooked and tossed with a touch of chopped chipotles in adobo and cilantro

JAPANESE Japanese rice is a short-grain white rice that has been polished. It must be cooked in a special way so it does not get mushy, and can be used as a side dish or in sushi.

JASMINE Jasmine rice is a polished white rice that cooks up pure white. Its long firm grains should be steamed and are slightly sticky, so they are easy to eat with chopsticks or a fork. Jasmine rice has a definite sweet perfume and is traditionally served with Asian dishes.

RED (MAHOGANY) A whole-grain Asian rice with a red coating, red rice is sometimes called cargo rice. Red rice tends to be sticky when cooked (it should be cooked Japanese-style) and has a pronounced nutty flavor.

WHITE White rice has had the nutritious outer layer polished off. After you taste some of the more interesting varieties of rice, white rice will seem boring. It can be steamed or cooked pilaf-, paella-, or Mexican-style.

WILD Wild rice is a type of grass, not a true rice. The long tough grains must be cooked gently for a long time in plenty of water, until they open up and bloom. Wild rice is always nutty tasting and very chewy; it is best combined with another more tender rice or grain.

HOW TO COOK RICE

STEAMED RICE Use a small, heavy-bottomed saucepan or stockpot with a tight-fitting lid. Bring the water to a boil, add a pinch of salt, if desired, and sprinkle in the rice. Shake the pan gently to evenly distribute the rice. Reduce the heat to medium-low, and cover. Cook for the amount of time indicated in the chart on page 174. Turn off the heat, fluff the rice gently with a fork, and replace the lid. Let the rice steam for 10 minutes.

RICE PILAF Sauté 1 tablespoon of minced onion in 1 teaspoon of olive oil. Add 1 cup of basmati or long grain rice and stir until the rice is golden and toasted. Add 1¾ cups of water or Basic Vegetable Stock (page 176), a pinch of salt, and a few threads of saffron, if you like. Bring to a boil, then cover, and cook on low heat until done, or cover and bake in a 350 degree F oven for 30 minutes. When cooked, fluff the rice with a fork, cover, and let stand for 10 minutes before serving.

MEXICAN-STYLE RICE In a dry skillet, toast 1 cup of long-grain brown rice until lightly golden. Sauté 1 tablespoon of minced onion with 1 clove of garlic, minced, until softened and add to the rice. Puree 1 cored

NATURAL SODIUM AND *UMAMI*

Flavor can be enhanced without the use of meat or salt. One way is to use glutamate-rich vegetables, such as mushrooms and seaweed, to give a full-rounded flavor that the Japanese call *umami*. Miso paste is also a source of flavor, but it is very high in salt.

Some vegetables, especially dark leafy greens and celery, have a naturally salty taste. Leafy greens may be used in salads or shredded and added to soups and stocks. Celery is an essential part of mirepoix, a combination of carrots, celery, and onion that forms the base for most soups, stocks, and stews. The stalks are most commonly used, but celery leaves make a terrific fresh-tasting garnish. Knobby celery root appears in fall. Peel and cook it with potatoes or winter stews, or shred it and combine with apples and walnuts for a classic Waldorf Salad. To prevent browning, dunk raw celery root in lemon and water.

tomato in a blender with ½ cup of water; add enough water to make 1¾ cups and pour over the rice. Stir, turn heat to low, cover, and cook for 25 minutes, or until all the liquid is absorbed. Fluff the rice, turn off the heat, cover, and let stand for 10 minutes. Some cooks add sautéed diced carrots, peas, or peppers to the rice at this point.

PAELLA-STYLE RICE WITH SOFRITO   In 2 teaspoons of olive oil, sauté 1 tablespoon minced onion, 2 tablespoons minced green pepper, and 1 large clove garlic, minced, until soft, stirring often. Add 1 Roma tomato, diced small, and cook briefly. Add 1 cup of long-grain rice (brown, converted, or basmati) and a pinch of salt, if desired. Cook, stirring, for 1 minute, then add the amount of water called for in the chart on page 174 depending on the type of rice you are using, and a couple of strands of saffron, if desired. Cover and cook for the indicated time, or until all the liquid is absorbed. Fluff with a fork, turn off the heat, cover, and let stand for 10 minutes.

JAPANESE-STYLE RICE   For best results, use imported Japanese or Calrose rice. Place the rice in a deep pan and wash with several changes of cold water until the water is mostly clear. Let the rice soak for 30 minutes, drain, and add the amount of water called for in the chart on page 174. Bring the rice to a boil, uncovered, then reduce the heat to low, cover, and cook for 15 minutes. Turn off the heat and let stand covered for 10 minutes. Fluff with a fork.

RISOTTO WITH BATTUTO   To make a basic risotto, sauté 1 tablespoon minced shallot or onion in 1 teaspoon of olive oil. Add ¾ cup arborio rice and cook, stirring, for 1 minute. Mix together 2 ¼ cups of water or Basic Vegetable Stock (page 176) and 2 tablespoons white wine, if desired. Add ½ cup of the liquid to the rice, stirring often as the rice absorbs the liquid. When the rice is almost dry, add another ½ cup of liquid and stir until absorbed. Repeat with the rest of the liquid; the rice should be thick, creamy, and cooked through but still firm. If you like, add a little grated Parmesan cheese or see Quick Variations for Rice (below) and serve hot.

WILD RICE   Bring the water to a boil, then add a pinch of salt and the wild rice. Cover and simmer over medium heat for 45 minutes, or until the grains have popped open. Drain off any excess liquid, and return the rice to the pot. Turn off the heat, cover, and let stand for 10 minutes. Wild rice is best combined with another type of firm long-grained rice or cooked grains.

RICE COOKING TIMES

	RICE	WATER	YIELD	COOKING TIME
ARBORIO	¾ cup	2⅓ cups	2 cups	30 minutes
BASMATI	1 cup	1¾ cups	3 cups	20 minutes
BROWN	1 cup	2¼ cups	3 cups	40 minutes
CHINESE BLACK	1 cup	1¾ cups	3 cups	30 minutes
CONVERTED	1 cup	2 cups	3 cups	25 minutes
JAPANESE	1 cup	1¼ cups	3 cups	25 minutes
JASMINE	1 cup	1½ cups	3 cups	12 minutes
RED (MAHOGANY)	1 cup	1¾ cups	3½ cups	30 minutes
WHITE	1 cup	2 cups	3 cups	20 minutes
WILD	1 cup	3 cups	3 cups	45 minutes

QUICK VARIATIONS FOR RICE

As with grains, rice is a perfect blank canvas for your culinary creativity.

✦ When cooking rice pilaf, add shallots, celery, carrots, mushrooms, garlic, fresh fennel, caramelized onions, or anything else that takes your fancy.

Or add a pinch of purchased spice blend when sautéing the onion. You could also substitute an Indian spice blend for the basmati long-grain rice.

✦ Fold leftover cooked vegetables into cooked rice. Grilled vegetables are especially delicious.

✦ Add some cooked large grains, such as wheat berries, or some colorful beans or legumes to cooked rice. Red beans, black beans, black-eyed peas, or red lentils are beautiful additions.

✦ Add grated fresh coconut and a squeeze of lime juice.

✦ Flavor with pureed vegetables or juices, such as orange, lemon, cranberry, tomato, beet, carrot, or pomegranate, by substituting juice for half the liquid.

✦ Stir citrus zest into the hot rice just before serving.

✦ Add a few tablespoons of pureed red pepper, chipotle, or other flavorful vegetables just before serving.

✦ Stir in a couple of tablespoons of chopped fresh herbs, cooked diced sweet peppers, or fresh tomatoes just before serving.

✦ Add roasted or fresh garlic.

✦ When fluffing steamed rice, stir in a handful of baby spinach leaves and a little chopped garlic. Replace the lid and steam for 10 minutes.

✦ Add cooked peas, edamame, or corn just before serving.

REAL FOOD VERSUS FAKE FOOD

In the past, so-called spa cuisine often went to elaborate lengths to whip up ersatz substitutes for foods like mayonnaise. These concoctions seldom fooled anyone. What has always made the Ranch different is founder Deborah's strong belief that almost any food—chocolate, oil, mayonnaise, whole-milk dairy products—can be enjoyed in moderation as part of a healthy diet based on fresh-picked organic vegetables, fruits, and whole grains.

At La Cocina, Jesús strives to teach his students how to cook "real" food that is healthy food. Processed foods should be avoided. Compare, for example, nonfat and regular cream cheese. The nonfat cream cheese is packed with stabilizers, gums, flavorings, and other ingredients with long names. The regular cream cheese on the other hand contains only milk, cream, and a culture. Unless you have allergies or strong food convictions, there's no reason why intrinsically healthy foods can't be enjoyed as you choose.

BASIC VEGETABLE STOCK

❈ MAKES 1 GALLON ❈

A flavorful vegetable stock subtly adds flavor to anything you make. Use herb stems, tomato trimmings, and vegetable stems and leaves in the stock. Celery root, kohlrabi, bell peppers, half a jalapeño, and any kind of fresh or dried mushrooms all work well. Don't use starchy vegetables, like potatoes, which cloud the stock, and strong-flavored herbs like rosemary, sage, oregano, or tarragon should be avoided. For more nutritional value, save vegetable cooking water uncovered for several days (refrigerated) instead of discarding it, and use it as part or all of the liquid.

2 WHOLE LEEKS

1 ONION

2 STALKS CELERY

4 CARROTS

½ TURNIP

1 BUNCH KALE OR COLLARD GREENS

1 WHOLE HEAD GARLIC, CUT IN HALF AROUND THE MIDDLE

4 TOMATOES, QUARTERED, OR 8 TOMATO CORES

½ BUNCH PARSLEY, WASHED

10 SPRIGS FRESH THYME

2 BAY LEAVES

10 BLACK PEPPERCORNS

6 LARGE DRIED SHIITAKES

1 GALLON PLUS 1 QUART WATER OR RESERVED VEGETABLE COOKING WATER

Wash and peel all the vegetables and cut roughly into 1-inch pieces. Place in a 3-gallon stockpot, add the water, and slowly bring to a simmer. Continue to simmer for 1 hour, or until the vegetables are very soft. Strain and into a clean stockpot or bowl discard the vegetables.

NOTE: Freeze stock in small containers and ice cube trays, or freeze flat in heavy-duty plastic freezer bags. Use pint or quart size, depending on your needs. They take up very little space and you always have a measured quantity of stock ready for soups and sauces.

BEANS AND LEGUMES

Dried beans, lentils, and peas (collectively known as legumes) are versatile and earthily satisfying, and they need almost no attention from you while they bubble away on a back burner or in a slow-cooker. Natural food stores carry an intriguing variety of shapes and sizes, each with its own unique flavor and color, including many delicious heirloom beans.

Working beans into your diet does take some planning, since larger beans may need up to 3 hours of cooking. A pressure cooker or slow-cooker would be useful if you cook beans often. If using canned beans, drain and rise them thoroughly.

Think outside the bowl. Make a bean salad, add cooked beans to green salads, mix a handful into cooked rice or grains, add to soups or use as a soup base, mash into refried beans to accompany Mexican food; or for a change of pace mash with lots of garlic and serve bubbling hot with tostaditas (see page 149) and raw vegetables.

BEANS, SMALL Includes black or turtle, pinto, adzuki, red, kidney, small white, navy, appaloosa, cranberry, cannellini, and other beans of this shape and size. These beans must be thoroughly cooked until they have a creamy texture. Use these beans in combination with rice or grains. Add to salads, soups, or stews, or mash them into a chunky puree to serve alongside Mexican food or as a dip.

BALANCING THE FLAVORS

When you taste food, think about what's missing. Do you want it to be more acidic? Sweeter? Hotter? Would a little bit of bitterness lend interest? Always cook to your taste.

TASTES FLAT	add a small amount of chopped fresh herbs, citrus, vinegar or salt
TOO SWEET	add salt or acid, add bitter
TOO VINEGARY	add a small amount of citrus juice and salt, add herbs
TOO BITTER	add small amount sweet and salt, and sometimes sour
TOO SALTY	the hardest to balance: add vinegar or citrus
TOO SPICY	add citrus, salt, bitter

BEANS, LARGE   Includes lima, fava, haba, and other dry broad beans, which are very large and firm after cooking. (Favas must be peeled after cooking.) Braise the cooked beans with aromatic vegetables and herbs as a side dish, mash into a puree or dip, or add to a stew. For an authentic tapa, chill and marinate large beans in any of the vinaigrettes in this book.

CHICKPEAS   Also known as garbanzos, chickpeas are high in protein. Add to a salad, toss with cooked pasta, or puree with garlic, lemon, and tahini to make hummus.

LENTILS, FLAT   Lentils are thin, flat, and disc-shaped, so they cook very quickly and take on the flavor of whatever they are cooked with. They come in a variety of colors—green, red, yellow, or brown. Lentils should be removed from the heat when they are cooked through but still firm, and are best served fresh and hot, rather than reheated. If you do cook them to mush, which is easy to do, simply turn them into a delicious soup.

LENTILS, ROUND   Gourmet lentils, such as black (caviar) or green (Puy) are tiny and round with great flavor and a unique appearance. These lentils cook in less than an hour and will keep their shape and firmness. Braise with savory vegetables and herbs and serve as a side dish, mix with grains or rice, or add whole to soups.

PEAS, SMALL   Includes black-eyed peas, mung beans, soybeans, and pigeon peas. This type of small bean cooks quickly, readily absorbs flavors from the broth, and has a crunchy, fresh taste. They are excellent in salads or mixed with rice.

PEAS, SPLIT   Split peas (called *dal* in India) are small and can be yellow, red, or green. Delicate, even crumbly, they they cook in a flash into a thick puree. Season and use as a pureed vegetable, or turn into a thick, sustaining soup.

HOW TO COOK LEGUMES

Pick over the beans carefully, removing stones or other foreign objects. Rinse the beans well under cold water and soak overnight, refrigerated, with just enough water to cover. Alternatively, you can bring the beans and water to a rolling boil, turn off the heat, and let stand for at least 1 hour. (Lentils and split peas do not need to be presoaked.) Drain off the soaking water, add the correct amount of fresh water according to the chart below, and bring the beans to a boil. Add any seasonings, such as a pinch of salt, a bay leaf, a few peppercorns, a peeled garlic clove, or slices of onion and celery.

Cover the pan, reduce the heat to low, and simmer until the beans are very tender but not dissolving. Add more water, if necessary, to just cover the beans. Cool the beans in the cooking liquid, uncovered (they will absorb quite a lot of liquid, and this keeps them moist and creamy inside). Serve right away or cover and refrigerate in their liquid. Beans taste as good the next day and will keep for several days in the refrigerator. Drain any excess liquid before serving.

BEAN AND LEGUME COOKING TIMES

	LEGUMES	WATER	YIELD	COOKING TIME
BEANS, SMALL	1 cup	5 cups	2$\frac{1}{2}$ cups	2 to 2$\frac{1}{2}$ hours
BEANS, LARGE	1 cup	5 cups	3 cups	2$\frac{1}{2}$ to 3 hours
CHICKPEAS	1 cup	5 cups	3 cups	2 to 2$\frac{1}{2}$ hours
LENTILS, FLAT	1 cup	4 cups	3 cups	30 to 40 minutes
LENTILS, ROUND	1 cup	4 cups	3 cups	50 minutes
PEAS, SMALL	1 cup	4 to 5 cups	2$\frac{1}{2}$ to 3 cups	40 to 60 minutes
PEAS, SPLIT	1 cup	4 cups	3 cups	20 minutes

CULINARY HERBS

Fresh herbs make a kitchen come alive. In summer, a countertop bouquet of fresh and flowering herbs from the garden inspires you as you cook. In winter, a sunny window full of potted herbs reminds us of the glory days of summer, and snippets of green herbs add life and zest to cold-weather cooking.

Most herbs taste vastly better fresh, with a few exceptions such as oregano, sage, savory, bay leaf, and thyme. All other dried herbs should be avoided. Why ruin your wonderful fresh flavors with dusty-tasting bottled green flecks? Never use dried or powdered garlic and onions either. Fresh is always better.

DEBORAH'S APPLE CIDER SYRUP

❋ MAKES 1 CUP ❋

This tangy-sweet syrup is one of Deborah Szekely's great ideas. Drizzle over pancakes, bananas, fruit, granola, a bit of cheese, or add to dressings and salads. Make a batch when fresh-pressed cider appears at the farmers' market. The rest of the year, use unfiltered organic cider.

2 CUPS FRESH UNFILTERED APPLE CIDER

2 TABLESPOONS BRANDY OR RUM

Into a 1½ quart saucepan, bring the cider to a boil. Reduce the heat to medium and continue to simmer until the cider has boiled down to a thin syrup—this may take as long as 30 minutes. You will see bubbles all across the surface when the syrup is ready. Add the brandy and set aside to cool.

When buying herbs, look for fresh-looking leaves and stems with no black or slimy areas. Set bunched herbs, like cilantro, parsley, or basil, upright in a glass of water, like a bouquet. Cover loosely with a plastic bag and refrigerate; they will keep for several days, and you can pick off a stem here and there as needed. Fresh herbs in plastic boxes should be stored in the box. Do not wash until just before use.

When herbs are in flower, pick off the tops and use in salads or desserts, or to decorate a plate. Add stalks of herb flowers to a simple bouquet of flowers for a fresh look and scent.

BASIL   Always used fresh, chopped, or crushed, at the very last minute. Genoese or Italian basil has the best flavor. Make pesto with Genoese basil only. Tres Estrellas grows other types—cinnamon, licorice, opal, lemon, and pineapple basil—that are more ornamental, with variegated, ruffled, and serrated leaves, and showy flowering tops. Add purple basil leaves to salad, place a layer of basil leaves in a vegetable terrine, use the flowers for garnish, toss a fruit salad with mint and cinnamon basil, add chopped lemon basil to fish dishes. Thai or "holy" basil makes a wonderful herb tea.

CHERVIL   Chervil looks like delicate, feathery parsley, but it has a potent anise flavor. In France, chervil is added to salad dressings, sauces, and omelets.

CHIVES AND CHIVE FLOWERS   Chives, including the pretty purple flowers, have a delicate onion scent and flavor. Snip the thin stems with scissors and sprinkle on almost anything.

CILANTRO (CORIANDER)   Cilantro is not native to Mexico, though it is associated with Mexican and Latin cooking in general. Many Asian cuisines make use of cilantro's brilliant taste as well. Cilantro grows easily, bolts quickly, and reseeds generously; it also grows well in pots. The seed, called coriander, has its own distinct flavor. Cilantro should be rinsed and kept refrigerated upright, with its stems in water, loosely covered. Chop just before using. Use it fresh, as in salsas, or stir it into hot food immediately before serving for a final garnish and dash of flavor. The stems are as flavorful as the leaves, so except for aesthetic, there is no reason not to use them.

DILL   Feathery dill has a sweet taste and is a natural match for seafood. Add to dressings, salads (especially potato salad), and anything with beets.

EPAZOTE   This herb grows wild through much of North and Central America, or seeds may be purchased online. Epazote is a large plant with sturdy, heavily serrated leaves. It will reseed itself indefinitely once established. The taste is reminiscent of both mint and oregano. It is generally used cooked, with black beans, potatoes, and seafood. Small snippets of

RASPBERRY VINEGAR

❊ MAKES ABOUT ½ CUP ❊

Use this recipe as a jumping-off point for making other kinds of fruit vinegars—peaches, figs, plums. Any other kind of berry, or mixed berries, may be substituted. Frozen berries may also be used. Recipe may be doubled.

1 CUP FRESH RASPBERRIES

½ CUP WHITE WINE VINEGAR

In a 1-quart saucepan, warm the vinegar and berries together over medium heat, mashing the berries with a small whisk. Remove from the heat and let stand for 30 minutes. Strain through a fine-mesh sieve, pressing down on the berries. Keep refrigerated and use within several days.

fresh epazote may be added to cheese quesadillas. A tea made from the leaves is used as digestive aid.

LAUREL Fresh bay leaf has a gentler flavor than the dried variety. It is lovely in stuffings or wrapped with fish in foil and grilled. Use in soups and stocks.

LAVENDER Both sweet and savory, beautiful lavender is a bee magnet in the garden and a hardy plant with many uses in your kitchen (and household). Lavender flowers scent teas and infusions; are delicious in dressings, sauces, and stuffings; and may be added to sorbets or tossed into a green salad.

LEMON VERBENA A sturdy bush with woody stems, verbena is a wonderful scented addition to any garden. It has a lush growth of shiny, narrow leaves and a potent lemon aroma. Tender leaves may be used to garnish green salads and fruit bowls, but the flavor is best when the leaves are crushed and infused into hot and iced teas, *aguas frescas*, sorbets, and sauces (be sure to strain before serving).

LEMONGRASS A hardy perennial that grows in subtropical areas, lemongrass may be purchased at any Asian market. The firm, white core can be minced and added to salsas, broths, teas, and sauces. The green outer leaves also make a delicious tea.

MARJORAM Sweet and delicious, marjoram has a taste similar to oregano but milder. Add to marinades for grilling and to salad dressings, or add small leaves right to a salad.

MINT Many kinds of mint (known in Mexico as *yerba buena*) will gladly take over your garden. Spearmint, peppermint, lemon mint, and Chef Jesús' favorite, licorice mint, are easy to grow and useful to have on hand. Try adding a touch of fresh mint to salad dressings, hot or iced teas, green salads, or hot or cold cooked grains, or sprinkle over cooked root vegetables such as carrots.

OREGANO Sharply spicy-sweet, with the taste of hot sun, oregano loves tomatoes, peppers, onions, olives and vinegar. It may be used fresh or dried. Greek oregano is stronger than Mexican oregano.

PARSLEY Either flat-leaf (Italian) or curly parsley may be used. Wash well and store upright in the refrigerator with its stems in water, loosely covered. Stem before chopping the leaves; stems may be added to stocks for extra flavor and nutrition. To make parsley taste better (and last longer in the refrigerator) place it in a fine sieve after chopping, and rinse well with cold water. Roll up in a clean linen towel and wring thoroughly. The parsley will be dry and fluffy.

ROSEMARY   Strongly resinous rosemary needs to be handled with care; the aroma is much more pleasant than the slightly bitter taste. Use only tender leaves for chopping. Whole tips may be used for stuffing, or tossed on the grill to scent grilled foods. Strong, slender branches make excellent decorative skewers.

SAGE   Fresh sage is warmly aromatic and complements anything roasted or grilled. Small amounts of sage can be chopped and added to stuffings. It also makes a soothing tea. Bundles of sage may be gathered, tied, and dried—scenting a room better than any potpourri. Wild sage is best, but any strong-smelling variety will do.

SAVORY   Closely related in taste to both sage and marjoram, the milder summer savory accents grilled and roasted foods and is wonderful in stuffings, on bread and pizzas, and on all vegetables.

SORREL   Sorrel looks like spinach, but tastes lemony and sharp. It is one of the first herbs of spring, when its tartness is welcomed. Sorrel is wonderful with fish and seafood, added to sauces or soups, or sautéed with other spring greens.

THYME   Thyme's tiny leaves pack great flavor. It is as useful dried as fresh, since its delicate herbal flavor changes very little when it is dried. Common varieties include lemon thyme and English thyme.

TARRAGON   A classic herb with fish, shrimp, eggs, salad dressings, and cold and hot sauces, tarragon should always be used fresh. It is often combined with chives and parsley or chervil in fines herbs, and makes exquisite vinegar. Delicate French tarragon has the best flavor.

VEGETABLE COOKING TECHNIQUES

Vegetables may be divided into two categories: those that grow above the ground, and those that grow beneath the ground. Vegetables that grow above the ground like to be cooked quickly—dropped into boiling water, stir-fried, or steamed. Vegetables that grow below the ground are best started in cold water, then roasted or otherwise slow-cooked.

MANDOLINE

A mandoline easily slices perfect rounds and julienne, and has many other uses. Consider investing in a good quality mandoline—it will save you time and add professional polish to everything you cook.

BAKE Cook with dry heat, such as in an oven (see Roast).

BLANCH Drop into briskly boiling water until cooked, then drain and plunge immediately into ice water to stop the cooking action. This method is usually used for green vegetables, because blanching will preserve a bright-green color. Blanch vegetables that you plan to add to salads, or wish to reheat later.

BRAISE Slow-cook food on a bed of aromatic vegetables with a small amount of liquid. Almost any vegetable can be braised, but leafy greens and root vegetables are especially good. Aromatic vegetables are sautéed. Vegetables to be braised are cut and seasoned lightly and a small amount of water or Basic Vegetable Stock (page 176)—just enough to moisten the bottom of the pan—is added. Cover and cook slowly over medium-low heat until the vegetables are soft, but not mushy: about 15 minutes for dark leafy greens, 30 minutes for root vegetables or kohlrabi.

BROILING Cook or brown no more than 3 inches from a heat source. Broiling is an alternative to grilling. It is also useful for cooking just the top of something, as in browning the top of a casserole or gratin or charring peppers. Watch constantly to prevent overcooking.

BROWN Expose the surface of food to heat, so it becomes brown in color and draws out new, delicious flavors. This may be done through direct contact, such as on a grill or in a sauté pan, or indirectly, by roasting at high heat or cooking under a broiler. Browning is also sometimes called caramelizing, though they are slightly different processes.

CARAMELIZE Brown the natural sugars in food by cooking in a heavy-bottomed pan over low to medium heat for 30 to 60 minutes, or until the food is soft (see photos at left). This technique works best with onions, carrots and beets, which are rich in natural sugars.

CHAR (see Roast) Cook until blackened, over a flame, on a grill, or under a broiler. Charring removes the skins from fresh chiles and bell peppers, and imparts a lovely smoky flavor.

GRATINÉE Cook overlapping slices of any kind of vegetable in a wide shallow dish until soft. An optional crust of breadcrumbs or cheese may be added and cooked until brown and bubbling.

GRILL Cook over direct or indirect heat from flame or coals. Grilled foods always look appetizing, and grilling has the advantage of being very simple to do. It also brings out the natural flavors of food and uses very little oil. You can grill eggplant, onions, asparagus, summer squash, and any other firm vegetables, including baby carrots and small potatoes. Firm fruits grill beautifully—figs, plums, nectarines, apricots, and pears in particular. A grill basket makes grilling smaller fruits and vegetables or seafood a little easier. Firm fish and seafood or tofu may be grilled, but be careful to cook over moderate heat and don't overcook. Foods to be grilled may be marinated or sprinkled with a dry spice rub prior to grilling.

It is possible to grill year-round no matter where you live. Outdoor grills may be fueled with propane, charcoal, or wood. Indoor grilling may be done very successfully in a heavy iron pan with a ridged bottom, or in a countertop electric grill, which cooks top and bottom simultaneously. The grill should always be very clean, and the grate should be lightly coated with oil—the food can also be lightly oiled or marinated—to prevent sticking.

PAN-ROAST   First sear, then place in a hot oven for a few minutes to cook the food all the way through. This technique is especially good with fish.

PUREE   Boil any vegetable until very soft, then place in a food processor and pulse until smooth. Purees add a smooth dab of brilliant color to sauces, dressings, rice, or mashed potatoes, and can even be used by themselves as a sauce. They can be thinned by adding some cooking liquid. For a perfectly smooth puree, push through a fine-mesh sieve with a rubber spatula. The vegetables for purees are hard squash, root vegetables, celery root, carrots, spinach, and beets. Fruits also make lovely purees.

ROAST   (see Char) Cook using dry heat so that the surface of the food is caramelized but the inside retains its moisture and flavor. Roasting is ideal for firm vegetables, such as potatoes, carrots, chayote, eggplant, turnips, and beets. Vegetables roast best when cut into 1½-inch chunks or wedges and tossed with olive oil and a small amount of salt. Cut vegetables should be spread out in one layer on a rimless baking sheet to roast evenly, and should take about 30 minutes in a preheated 400 degree F oven, but the time will vary depending on the type of vegetable and the accuracy of your oven. It's best to roast softer vegetables separately from harder vegetables because the cooking times will vary.

SAUTÉ   Cook quickly in a small amount of oil so that the food does not steam and release any liquid. Only quick-cooking foods, such as shrimp,

mushrooms or summer squash, should be sautéed. The technique is the same, regardless of the ingredients. If you are cooking a lot of food, don't overcrowd the pan—cook in batches, instead, or use two pans. If you are sautéing different types of vegetables, keep them separate and add the hardest ones first, then, after a few minutes, the softer vegetables. Seasonings such as salt, pepper, lemon, or soft herbs can be added at the end.

SEAR   Cook oiled food in a very hot pan to form a caramelized crust. Searing does not cook food, it just gives it some color and a smoky flavor. (See also Pan-roast.) When searing, lightly oil the food to be cooked, don't put the oil in the pan—that's frying. Add the food to the pan in one layer and don't touch the food until it has some color from the hot pan, then it may be turned once (see scallops at left).

SIMMER   Cook in liquid kept just below the boiling point. Simmering develops the flavor of stocks, soups, and stews without cooking off all the liquid. It is gentler than boiling, which can toughen or break up food. To simmer, reduce the heat under the pot until the surface is barely moving and only a few bubbles can be seen. Do not cover.

STEAM   Cook food over boiling water, stock, or spice-infused broth. Steaming is a great way to cook delicate foods such as fish. You can cook a whole meal in a steamer basket, with layers of aromatic vegetables beneath fish or shrimp.

STIR-FRY   Cook uniform pieces of food quickly over very high heat in a small amount of oil. Foods to be stir-fried should be reasonably tender (potatoes, for example, are not suitable) and must be cut into small pieces, thin slices, or long thin sticks to create a maximum amount of surface area so they cook quickly when they come in contact with the hot wok. Summer squash, peppers, onions, shrimp, mushrooms, bean sprouts, shredded greens, and cabbage are all ideal for stir-fries. To stir-fry, heat a large heavy-bottomed sauté pan or wok over medium-high heat until a drop of water dances on the surface. Add a small amount of vegetable or light sesame oil and swirl to coat the pan. Immediately add any seasoning, such as onions, garlic, and ginger to the pan, and stir to flavor the oil. Once you can smell your seasonings, it's time to add the vegetables. Stir the vegetables continuously and toss with a wok shovel or spoon; the food must be kept moving at all times (see bottom photos at left). When the vegetables are just wilted, remove the wok from the heat and stir in a small amount of hoisin or soy sauce, if desired, and garnish with sliced green onions and a sprinkle of sesame seeds.

"IF YOU DIDN'T KNOW YOUR AGE,
HOW OLD WOULD YOU BE?"
SATCHEL PAIGE

THE SPA

Ranch spa treatments in the 1940s consisted entirely of fresh Tecate air, exercise on the hills and in the grape arbor, delicious fresh food (all vegetarian in those days) and lots of rest. These elements are still the most important part of looking and feeling your best, and are the focus of the Ranch week. But for any little rough edges that still need polishing, the Ranch excels in luxurious spa treatments—massages, facials, body scrubs, and full-tilt pampering—based on simple natural products, and often scented with the smells of the Ranch gardens: rosemary, lavender, lemon balm, and sage. ✦ A reminder: Everything in this chapter is for *external* use only—including the vodka skin toner on page 193. Be gentle with all treatments—no hard scrubbing—and if you have sensitive skin, test a small amount on the inside of your arm.

ABOUT HERBS

The plants and herbs mentioned in this chapter have been used for millennia; they are generally acknowledged as being mild and safe to use in small quantities *externally*.

Herbs and plant extracts have a history of medical use that is as old as the human race. Most of these products may be bought off the shelf. That does not mean they are all benign or harmless. Far from it! Many herbs and extracts have potent effects on the body and all should be used with respect and care. Rattlesnake venom is 100 percent natural and organic—but that doesn't mean it is safe! Sage essential oil is so powerful that in very small doses it can cause liver damage.

If the therapeutic use of herbs is of interest to you, talk to a medical professional before embarking on any course of herbs.

ESSENTIAL OILS

Essential oils have been described as "the soul of a plant." Enormous amounts of leaves or flowers are distilled to make a very small amount of essential oil. For example, an ounce of rose essential oil requires 2,000 pounds of rose petals; half an ounce of lemon verbena essential oil requires 15 wheelbarrow loads of the plant.

Essential oils are extremely potent and may provoke strong reactions in some people; proceed with caution. A few tiny drops of diluted oil are all you need to add a lovely scent—calming, invigorating, soothing, or sexy—to body scrubs and baths. Essential oils are never eaten or applied directly to the skin, but are diluted with another type of neutral oil (such as almond oil) before use. Fresh or dried herbs and flowers may be used in place of oils.

Be sure to buy essential oils from a reliable source. Oils are very expensive and there exists the temptation to adulterate oils through dilution with imitation products. Beware, too, of imitation oils, which are made in the laboratory out of chemicals and have never been near a plant. These less-expensive imposters may smell almost real, at first, but it's like love—only the real thing will do.

INFUSIONS, DECOCOTIONS, TINCTURES, TISANES, AND BALMS

INFUSION   Pour boiling water over fresh or dried herbs or flowers, steep until cool (or for a set period of time), and strain. Teas and tisanes are infusions.

DECOCTION   Plant material such as roots, bark, seeds, or dried berries are simmered for a period of time and strained. Natural dyes are made in this way.

DISTILLATION OF ESSENTIAL OIL   Plant material—lots of it—is placed in a specially designed container that allows steam to be introduced. The steam breaks open the cell walls of the plants. Inside the cells are aromatic compounds, which combine with the steam. The steam is collected in a cooling chamber where it condenses into droplets of liquid, called a hydrosol, which contains the watery part of the plant. Essential oils float to the top of the hydrosol and are drawn off.

TINCTURE   An herb or flower is immersed in alcohol for a set period of time. The active compounds and benefits of the plant dissolve in the alcohol, which is then strained off.

BALM   A creamy or waxy material that has been infused, at some point, with an herb extract for scent or other properties. Also called a salve.

ALOE VERA

A useful plant to have around is the aloe vera, often called "the burn plant." There are hundreds of types of aloe, all native to Africa, but only *a. vera barbadensis* is used medically. The fleshy gooey leaves of aloe vera are high in water and contain many vitamins and minerals. The sticky gel inside the leaves has antiseptic and antibiotic properties and is effective for treating external skin conditions such as minor burns, skin infections, ulcerations, and hives. To use, cut a small piece from a live leaf, split open, and apply directly to the affected area. Aloe extracts are not as effective as the live plant, which will thrive indoors in a sunny window, or outdoors all year round in mild climates. Spring visitors to the Ranch are treated to the sight of orange clouds hovering over the ground, the aloe in bloom.

CALENDULA BALM

❋ MAKES 1 1/2 CUPS ❋

Rows of bright yellow calendula flowers grow thickly clustered along the pathways of the garden. Their sunny glow is more than mere beauty; herbalists swear by calendula's soothing and healing properties. Rub this soothing balm into rough skin or scaly patches. Calendula flowers may be dried and turned into handsome bouquets or woven into straw wreaths, a reminder of summer's glory.

1 CUP CALENDULA FLOWER PETALS

1 CUP OLIVE OR ALMOND OIL

1/2 CUP SHEA BUTTER

1/4 CUP BEESWAX

1. Place the calendula petals in a clean glass jar. Pour the oil over, cover, and set in a sunny window for one week to infuse the oil. Strain, pressing down on the petals; discard the petals.

2. Place the shea butter and beeswax in a small saucepan and melt over very gentle heat, stirring often. Add the infused calendula oil and stir to combine. Pour the mixture into sterilized 4-ounce glass jars and cover with sterlizied lids. The balm will thicken overnight.

DRYING HERBS AND FLOWERS

If you are interested in making your own potpourris, herbs teas, and dried spice blends, consider investing in an inexpensive dehydrator. This method will quickly dry fresh herbs and flowers while preserving color and flavor. Bundles of herbs may be dried, upside down, in a cool area free of dust and insects. Only some herbs, such as bay leaf, thyme, oregano, marjoram, sage, and savory, are really suitable for drying. For more on herbs, see page 179. Flowers such as rose buds and rose petals, calendula, and lavender may be dried.

RANCHO LA PUERTA
AT-HOME SKIN CARE REGIME

Rancho La Puerta's skin care guru is Jan Greaves, an ageless beauty with perfect skin. Jan urges guests to keep it basic and natural; the following easy regime is one she designed, using simple food-based products, for guests to use at home.

✦ Before using any skin treatment, know your skin type and condition. Consult with a dermatologist if you have allergies or a skin condition.

✦ Be gentle! If anything feels uncomfortable, stop immediately and rinse thoroughly with tepid water.

✦ Avoid extremes of temperature: Use tepid water for rinsing, and be careful with steam treatments.

✦ Always wear sunscreen on exposed skin (including the hands) and a hat.

JAN'S BASIC AT-HOME CARE
FOR ALL SKIN TYPES

CLEANSING   Apply 2 or 3 tablespoons of plain yogurt, which is very soothing, to damp skin and massage well over face and throat area. Rinse well with 15–20 splashes of tepid water.

TONING   Stir 1 teaspoon organic apple vinegar into 8 ounces of water (dilute more if your skin is sensitive.) Apply to face and throat with cotton pads in an upward sweeping motion. This restores a normal pH to the skin. *To treat blemished or erupted skin,* mix 2 ounces grapefruit juice with 2 ounces vodka and 3 ounces mineral water. Apply to skin. The vitamins in the grapefruit juice will dry the blemishes, and the vodka tightens the pores.

NOURISHING   While skin is till damp, apply one of the following to dry areas only:

✦ A light application of any cold-pressed oil, such as olive oil.

✦ A light application of fresh mayonnaise: with a whisk or fork, slowly beat 1 cup olive oil into 1 large egg yolk. Add 1 teaspoon fresh lemon juice. Store in the refrigerator; this is a wonderful moisturizer.

✦ A thin layer of organic-source margarine, without added color or flavoring.

EXFOLIATION A necessary step for removing the accumulation of dead cells, this procedure should not be used on areas of active acne. Exfoliation can be done daily, or once or twice a week depending on skin type.

Several products may be used for exfoliation such as sea salt, yellow corn-meal, and white sugar. White sugar is preferred because of its antibacterial properties. The same scrub may be made in larger quantities and used for a body scrub.

In a small bowl, make a paste by adding water, a teaspoon at a time, to about 2 tablespoons of fine sea salt, cornmeal, or white sugar to make a soft, spreadable paste. (Don't add too much, or the product will dissolve.) Gently massage the mixture over the entire face and neck area with the tips of the fingers to loosen debris from the skin. Finish by rinsing well with warm water, followed by a cold splash. If you like, a few drops of lavender oil may be added to the mixture.

MASKS

To achieve the most benefits a gentle steaming of the face should be done first. Simply toss a few bags of chamomile tea or lavender into a pot of boiling water. Pour the water into a bowl or sink and tent your head with a towel to capture the steam. Enjoy the steam for several minutes, then proceed with a mask suitable for your skin type.

FOR OILY SKIN

FOR CLEARING UP OILY SKIN   Mix 1 egg white with 1 tablespoon fresh lemon juice and 1 tablespoon plain yogurt. Apply to a cleansed face and let dry for 20 minutes. Remove with warm water and follow with a moisturizer.

FOR HEALING A BLEMISHED COMPLEXION   Soak 1 slice white bread and 1 teaspoon fresh yeast in ¼ cup milk and mix into a paste. Apply to skin. Leave on for 30 minutes. Remove with warm water, then moisturize.

TO REDUCE INFLAMMATION   Apply plain yogurt lightly over entire face and leave on for 30 minutes. Remove with a warm, soft washcloth.

FOR COMBINATION SKIN

EGG MASK   The perfect mask for combination skin. Separate 1 egg and beat the white and yolk separately. Cover the dry areas with the yolk, and the oily parts with the white. Leave on for 20 minutes. Remove with warm water and follow with moisturizer.

CLARIFYING TREATMENT MASK   Mix 1 tablespoon finely ground almonds, 1 tablespoon honey, and 1 egg white. Apply and leave on for 15 minutes. Remove by massaging with warm water in a circular motion over skin, rinse well, and follow with moisturizer.

FOR LOOSENING BLACKHEADS   Cook 2 tablespoon barley with enough water to cover, until very soft. Make a paste. Apply to skin while still warm and leave on for 15 minutes. Remove with a damp, soft face cloth, or by splashing with warm water. This is also useful for breakouts on the back.

ALOE VERA MASK   Combine 2 tablespoons brewer's yeast powder, 1 tablespoon aloe vera juice, and 1 egg white. Apply to skin and leave on for 20–30 minutes. Remove with warm water. This mask will also heal blemishes and soothe irritated skin.

FOR DRY SKIN

TO RE-TEXTURIZE THE SKIN   Pour 4 ounces boiling water over a handful of rosemary branches and steep for 20 minutes. Strain and cool completely. Mix with 2 egg whites and 2 teaspoons powdered milk. Apply to face and leave on for 20 minutes. Remove with a damp, soft face cloth or warm water splash.

HEALING HERBAL MASK   Combine 2 tablespoons avocado oil and 2 tablespoons wheat germ oil. Heat very gently over simmering water until warm. Test on your wrist to make sure it is not too hot. Apply to face and neck and leave on for 20 minutes. The oil may be left on the skin, or removed with warm water.

SOOTHING AVOCADO MASK   Mix 1 tablespoon wheat germ oil with ½ mashed avocado. Apply to skin and relax for 20–30 minutes as it nourishes the skin. The vitamin E in the avocado will do wonders for the skin. Remove with a damp, soft washcloth or a warm water splash.

BANANA MASK FOR DRY PATCHES   Puree 1 peeled banana with 1 tablespoon olive oil. Apply on extra dry, scaly patches and leave on for 20–30 minutes. Remove with a damp face cloth or warm water splash.

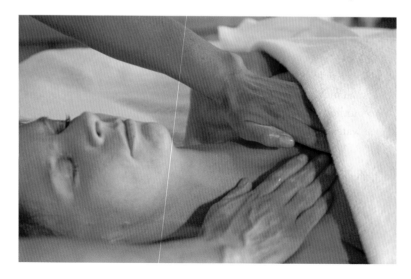

BODY TREATMENTS

Climb in the shower and, using a bath mitt, gently scrub yourself all over with one of these easy treatments, then rinse with warm (not hot) water. The coarse material exfoliates; the oils and other ingredients condition the skin. Don't use coarse exfoliators such as sea salt on inflamed skin or areas of active breakouts. Note: use an unbreakable container, and be careful—the oils can make the shower slippery.

BROWN SUGAR–HONEY–FLOWER SCRUB   Combine 1 cup brown sugar, ¼ cup honey, ¼ cup almond oil, and 2 teaspoons fresh flower petals or 1 teaspoon dried flower petals, such as rose, lavender, or calendula. A few drops of your favorite essential oil may be substituted. Scrub with a bath mitt, then rinse. Look out for bees!

YOGURT BODY RUB   Massage plain yogurt (which contains lactic acid) into your skin. Leave on for several minutes, then shower off with warm water.

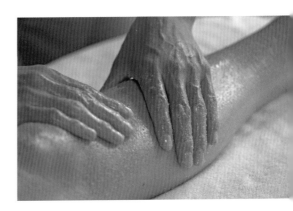

SEA SALT SCRUB   Mix a handful of sea salt with a few drops of essential oil, such as grapefruit. Scrub the salt mixture all over, then shower off.

EUCALYPTUS-ROSEMARY BATH INFUSION   Stuff a good handful of tender rosemary branches and a few eucalyptus leaves into a small bag made of muslin, or wrap in cheesecloth and tie securely. Toss into the bath while it is running and let it steep for several minutes. Remove and enjoy. The same technique may be used with chamomile or green tea leaves.

JAN'S PEPPERMINT PEDICURE SOAK   Soothe tired feet, or soak your feet before a pedicure. Combine 4 ounces finely ground oatmeal, 4 ounces rice milk powder, and 4 drops of peppermint essential oil. Place in a small muslin bag and secure the top. Place the bag in a foot basin and pour hot water over the bag and let it steep for several minutes. Add warm water to come up over the ankles and soak the feet for 20 minutes.

ALMOND MANICURE OIL   Soak your hands in warm water with a small amount of fresh lemon juice for 10 minutes. Combine equal amounts of almond oil and vitamin E oil, and massage into cuticles and nails.

ACKNOWLEDGMENTS

¡GRACIAS!

Knowing that so many people today lack the complete calorie approach to food led me to create this book with so many remarkable colleagues.

My daughter, Sarah Livia Brightwood, connected the kitchens of Rancho La Puerta and fresh organic foods by reviving an old farm, Tres Estrellas, and turning it into one of the world's premier organic gardens. She designed La Cocina Que Canta (The Kitchen that Sings) to sit in a garden that invites students to pick some of their own ingredients before each hands-on class. Sarah is Rancho La Puerta's landscape designer, artistic soul, guardian of nature, and community activist.

I was thrilled to find writer and chef Deborah Schneider. Her previous cookbook, *!Baja! Cooking on the Edge*, captured the raw energy and spirit of Rancho La Puerta's homeland, a region some still consider *la frontera* (frontier). The higher cuisines of Mexico don't come into play much along this crooked, thousand-mile peninsula. Simpler foods, usually fresh from the grill, infuse our border and peninsular culture, and at Rancho La Puerta we honor this simplicity. By interviewing our chefs, walking the rows of our organic farm, and testing testing testing, Deborah has captured the Ranch's newest approach to healthful cuisine in these pages.

I am very proud of Chef Jesús González. I plucked him from the Golden Door, where he grew up under the tutelage of the great chef Michel Stroot. Jesús now teaches several classes a week at La Cocina Que Canta, the first spa resort cooking school of its kind. Every few weeks he is joined by a talented guest chef from the ranks of America's best-known teachers, cookbook authors, and television personalities.

The school's director, Antonia Allegra, has played another vital role in this book. Her culinary knowledge, gentle wisdom, and wide-ranging connections (she is past-president of the International Association of Culinary Professionals, as well as the originator of the world-renowned Symposium for Professional Food Writers held each year at The Greenbrier in West Virginia) have helped propel the Ranch's cooking school to the forefront of culinary destinations.

Rancho La Puerta's nutritionist, Yvonne Nienstadt, has also helped guide these recipes to fruition. And our Tres Estrellas gardener, Salvador Tinajero, is a treasure. Every plant at the farm thrives on his energy—and so do the Ranch guests.

Finally, everywhere you turn, the steady hand of our general manager, Roberto Arjona, stays the course and inspires the staff to believe in *siempre mejor*.

Deborah Szekely

THANK YOU

The engaging, energetic spirit behind this book is that of Deborah Szekely. For many years I had known *of* her, and her fascinating life and multi-faceted career. Having the opportunity to work *with* her was the chance of the lifetime, and I thank her for allowing me to be part of this project. Deborah's creative energy is a constant inspiration. And her fearless insistence, over the years, on following her beliefs is a lesson in personal courage.

Sarah Livia Brightwood, Deborah's talented daughter, is the driving force behind the miracle that is Tres Estrellas. I can't wait to see what she comes up with next. Chef Jesús González provided much of the inspiration and most of the raw recipes for this book.

Tres Estrellas' farm manager, Salvador Tinajero, the wizard of the garden and a force of nature in his own right. Antonia Allegra, director of La Cocina Que Canta, contributed many hours and thoughtful suggestions to the compilation and shaping of the book.

Ranch nutritionist Yvonne Nienstadt (a chef herself) was most helpful with the original recipes. Special thanks to Peter Jensen and to Roberto Arjona and his incredible staff. *¡Muchissimo gracias!*

Heartfelt thanks to literary agent Carole Bidnick of Bidnick & Company and to Leslie Stoker, vice president of Stewart, Tabori & Chang. Editor Luisa Weiss of STC is a pleasure to work with and her sure-handed, patient guidance has made this a much better book. The gorgeous photography by Robert Holmes and Andrea Johnson was a gift. Thank you! Anna Christian, our designer, pulled it all together into a beautiful book.

Last, but certainly not least, I wish to acknowledge the special place that is Rancho La Puerta, which fairly glows with the joyous energy of six decades.

Deborah Schneider

I want to thank everyone who made this book possible and special thanks to the following people for all of their support and encouragement: Sra. Deborah Szekely and Sarah Livia Brightwood for believing in me and giving me the opportunity that has changed my life. Roberto Arjona, General Manager of Rancho La Puerta. My Mom and Dad, Emelia González and Jesús González Sr. My wife, Rosa, and my sons—Abraham, Isaac, Xavier—everything I do is because you are my inspiration. Lorena Gonzalez, my little sister. Yvonne Nienstadt—thank you for analyzing my recipes. Deborah Schneider, author of the book. Antonia Allegra, my coach—I have learned so much from you. Merrilee Olsen Axtell, food testing. Salvador Tinajero, our Head Gardener. Roma Maxwell, Peter Jensen, and Aida Alibegovic of Rancho La Puerta. Michelle Stroot, my mentor. And of course special thanks to my support team at culinary school: Rene Gonzalez and team Ana, Celia, Griselda, Elizabeth, Francisco, Lizzeth, and Alejandro.

Jesús González

INDEX

Page references in *italic* refer to illustrations.

Nuts, 130

O

Oats, in summery nectarine and berry
    tartlets, *66, 73*
Oils:
    essential, 190, 191
    nut, 99
    olive, 101, 130
    reducing intake of, 130
Oily skin, treatments for, 195–96
Olive oil, 101, 130
Orange(s):
    broiled, with honey yogurt and
        pistachios, 145
    saffron pine-nut bread, 29
Oregano, 179, 182, 192
Organic foods, 14, 37, 130

P

Paella:
    lobster and shrimp, *50, 54–55, 55*
    -style rice with sofrito, 173
Paige, Satchel, 188
Paletas, 35
Pan-roasting, 185
Pansies, 57
Papaya, avocado sorbet in, with aged
    balsamic vinegar, *47, 47*
    Parchment, mixed seafood steamed in,
        with shallots and white wine, *42, 45*
Parsley, 180, 182–83
Parsnips, in root vegetables roasted with
    honey, balsamic, and spices, 138
Pasilla chiles, 40
Pasta:
    butternut squash gnocchi, 22
    pesto linguine with lemon zest, sun-dried
        tomato, and snow peas, 46
Peach, blackberry, and plum sorbets, trio
    of, 56
Peanuts, coconut ice with chocolate drizzle
    and, 125
Pear(s):
    carrot and ginger soup with, 98
    roasted, and arugula salad with
        pomegranate-chipotle vinaigrette,
        158, 159
    strudel with brown sugar cream, 115
Peas (legumes), 178, 179

Pedicure soak, peppermint, Jan's, 197
Pepper(s) (bell):
    jicama slaw, spicy, with mint-jalapeno
        dressing, 123
    Mediterranean saffron stew with
        lemon zest aioli, *110, 113*
    Mediterranean salad, 52
    red, and shrimp on rosemary sprigs, *18, 21*
    red, cucumber, dill, and yogurt salad
        with, 60
    roasted, grilled white corn soup with
        leeks and, 68
    roasted, polenta gratin with braised fall
        greens, goat cheese and, *104, 107–8*
    roasting, 108
Peppermint pedicure soak, Jan's, 197
Pesto linguine with lemon zest, sun-dried
    tomato, and snow peas, 46
Phyllo (dough):
    beggars' purses, exotic mushroom and
        spinach, *96,* 100–101
    glazed roasted salmon en croûte, 137
    pear strudel with brown sugar cream, 115
Picante sauce, *90,* 91
Pico de gallo, 89, *90*
Pilaf, rice, 172, 174–75
Pineapple-carrot cake with apricot cream
    frosting, 139
Pine-nut orange saffron bread, 29
The Pink Menu, 74–82
Pistachios:
    bananas flambé with chocolate and, 103
    broiled oranges with honey yogurt
        and, 145
    lemon verbena rice pudding with fresh
        fruit and, 93
Planning ahead, 169
Plum, blackberry, and peach sorbets, trio
    of, 56
Polenta, 168
    gratin with braised fall greens, goat
        cheese, and roasted bell peppers,
        104, 107–8
Pomegranate-chipotle vinaigrette, *158, 159*
Ponche, 148
Popsicles, Mexican (*paletas*), 35
Portion control, 14
La Posada (menu), 146–55
Potato:
    kohlrabi gratin with garlic and white

        truffle oil, 161
    new, salad with chervil and shallots, 72
Processed foods, 37, 175
Pureeing, 185

Q

Quiche, mushroom, with goat cheese, 131–32
Quick Weekday Dinner (menu), 140–45
Quince-apple *mermelada* tartlets, 109
Quinoa, 167, 168
    black, tabbouleh, 64

R

Raspberry vinegar, 181, *181*
Real food vs. fake food, 175
Red rice, Mexican, 153
Rice, 170–75
    cooking, 172–74
    eight fast meals based on, 171
    lobster and shrimp paella, *50, 54–55, 55*
    pudding, lemon verbena, with fresh
        fruit and pistachios, 93
    quick variations for, 174–75
    red, Mexican, 153
    varieties of, 170–72
Ricotta:
    cheesecake with berries and lavender,
        30, *31*
    creamy honeyed, grilled figs with
        almonds and, *65, 65*
Risotto with battuto, 174
Roasting, 185
Romaine hearts and escarole with
    kalamata olives, toasted pine nuts,
    and creamy Asiago dressing, 112
Root vegetables roasted with honey,
    balsamic, and spices, 138
Rose geranium flowers, 57
Rosemary and rosemary flowers, 57, 183
    eucalyptus bath infusion, 197
    re-texturizing treatment for dry skin, 196
    shrimp and red peppers on sprigs, *18, 21*
Roses, 57, 190, 192
Rum–roasted banana sorbet, 102
Rutabaga, in root vegetables roasted with
    honey, balsamic, and spices, 138

S

Saffron:
    orange pine-nut bread, 29